Audrey Evans, an Australian Aboriginal of the Gunggari/Kunja tribal language group, was also known by her Aboriginal name 'Kuloin', which means Black Swan. Together with her husband, David, who passed away in 1987, she raised four children. Following his death, and with almost no previous education, she started studying at fifty-five years of age.

Audrey gained a Bachelor of Arts degree and a Graduate Diploma of Adult and Vocational Education from Griffith University and went on to teach English, History and Aboriginal Cultural Studies with the Queensland Education Department. She lectured at Australian Catholic University, and as an active member of the advisory committee for Weemala, the Indigenous unit at Australian Catholic University, Audrey was instrumental in contributing to the growth of Indigenous students at the university.

In 1999 Audrey was selected to receive the National Aboriginal and Islander Day of Observance Committee Award, Indigenous Scholar of the Year. This award was granted in recognition of the number of Indigenous students Audrey helped to complete further study.

Many Lifetimes formed part of a Master of Arts in Creative Writing at the University of Queensland. Sadly, Audrey passed away in 2000 before she could see her memoir published.

Many Lifetimes

A Memoir

Audrey Evans

BANTAM
SYDNEY AUCKLAND TORONTO NEW YORK LONDON

MANY LIFETIMES
A BANTAM BOOK

First published in Australia and New Zealand in 2006
by Bantam

Copyright © Estate of Audrey Evans, 2006

All rights reserved. No part of this publication may be reproduced, stored in a retrieval system, transmitted in any form or by any means, electronic, mechanical, photocopying, recording or otherwise, without the prior written permission of the publisher.

National Library of Australia
Cataloguing-in-Publication Entry

Evans, Audrey, 1933–2000
Many lifetimes

IBSN 9 78186325 4793
ISBN 1 86325 479 X.

1. Evans, Audrey, 1933–2000. 2. Women, Aboriginal Australian – Biography. 3. Aboriginal Australians – Biography. I. Title.

920.00929915

Transworld Publishers,
a division of Random House Australia Pty Ltd
20 Alfred Street, Milsons Point, NSW 2061
http://www.randomhouse.com.au

Random House New Zealand Limited
18 Poland Road, Glenfield, Auckland

Transworld Publishers,
a division of The Random House Group Ltd
61–63 Uxbridge Road, Ealing, London W5 5SA

Random House Inc
1745 Broadway, New York, New York 10036

Typeset by Midland Typesetters, Australia
Printed and bound by Griffin Press, Netley, South Australia

10 9 8 7 6 5 4 3 2 1

Pseudonyms have been used and other details altered where necessary to protect the names and identities of people and organisations mentioned in this book.

Foreword

by Leah Purcell

Tribally, I would call Audrey Evans 'Aunty' as we are descendants of the Gunggari of Central South West Queensland; our 'Country' we visited as strangers, the traditional lifestyle we did not know – but Blackfella way, we still family. A woman I'll never meet, she's gone now, so I'll speak to her spirit, a need for me because Aunty spoke to my spirit in the giving of her story. With great respect, sincerity and pride I write this.

Ma (thank you) I say. I say Ma!

Aunty, the frankness, openness and honesty of your yarn goes beyond belief. You pulled no punches and often in the read you left me breathless. But I still eagerly turned the pages.

No one, not even the greatest of writers could dream up your truth, often stranger and always more harrowing than fiction, and without doubt your story will touch all who go with you on this, your amazing journey of Many Lifetimes.

It's not a complaint is it, Aunty? That's just the way it was – an era in which just being a female you were a second-class citizen, let alone suffering from an illness that had no diagnosis in those days but a shot of brandy and shock treatment. The confusion at those feelings, your mixed parentage and out of that the confusion as to who you were, as to where you sat in this picture called 'Life' that revolved around you and that you travelled through. But in your writing it was never a burden, just a life lived, dealing with the hand you were dealt, hey Aunty? And oh boy, what a hand!

I hung on tight to the pages as my anxiety rose, I willed your strength to hold up, your strength immeasurable. Your good times, your adventurous free spirit brought great laughs and I laughed out loud, and when your soul was broke I cried hard, but my tears were dried as I rode with you on the winds of freedom that that pony provided. With kindness you spoke of those you loved and those who did not deserve it, but you unconditionally gave it. You had great respect for your gentle dear mother and for those who helped you along the way. Your dignity and integrity rose, but you weren't perfect and you said so. Your love of poetry can be heard in your words as you describe your days, and your description is all too real.

I was with you on your journey, transported on the pages of your book. A piece of Australian literature, told to allow understanding of a time in which Audrey Evans lived and survived.

I can only hope that before your passing you found your peace and your spirit has moved on to your next journey.

A gift so great as understanding, I thank you for giving me yours: an era that is my history as an Australian woman, a woman of the twenty-first century, a Gunggari umbi, a black woman of today's society. This story, given for the young and old, for all peoples, this story has been told. But for your bravery to put pen to paper and open your soul, I applaud and give you utmost respect.

Maybe we'll meet in the 'Dreaming', and when we do we'll sit down, sit in silence as only those who have shared an experience can do.

Prologue

This is my autobiography.

This is my story.

This is how my life has been so far – long and difficult and long and good.

I have wanted to write this story, this story of my life, my self, for myself, for many years.

It is a difficult task, the writing and the life, there are many sad and terrible and terrifying things, and I remember them, not as facts or events but as myself, like my skin or my hands; these memories are physical, and they are not in the past, they are here with me as I write and as I live.

And there are good memories, years and years of them – my children, my friends, my work, and now, late in my life, my Aboriginality, our struggle, which I have been part of all my life, suffering and surviving.

People say it is a great life, a heroic life, an important

story, one among the many that must be told if we are to know who we are, if I am to know who I am.

But I know who I am, I say, I have always known.

1993

Graduation Day

It was 1 March 1993. I stood in the wings of the Performing Arts Complex, wearing the blue academic gown and mortarboard of Griffith University, waiting my turn to walk across the stage. I was there to receive a Bachelor of Arts degree, and I was aware that I was an old woman, older than most of the other graduates who were with me that day. I was fifty-nine years of age. Yet at that moment I was as excited as a teenager in her first party dress.

I thought of my parents, and wished they could be there. They would have been so proud of me.

∞

My parents had been dead for a very long time. They had not lived to see the achievements of any of their children. My father died thinking that none of us would ever amount to anything worthwhile, because we were Aboriginals. He had told each of us from a very young age that Aboriginal people had bad blood. He told his two stepchildren, Robert and Beryl, and all of us – his own eight children – that we were incapable of learning beyond elementary level because Aboriginal people were not as bright as white people. Not until my father was dead did any of his children have the courage or self-confidence to allow their natural talents to emerge. At fifty-nine, I had come a long way from the schools of outback Queensland.

I tried to smile as I walked out onto the stage, but my face was rigid from trying to hold back the tears of happiness. I looked up to the balcony where three of my children, Yasmin, Jason and Debbie, sat excitedly videotaping my graduation. Although I was happy to see them there, I felt a little disappointed too, as none of my sisters or brothers had come. I was the only one in my family who had reached Year Twelve or beyond, and I felt saddened that my achievements appeared to mean so little to them.

As I looked out over the sea of white faces and blue mortarboard-capped students seated in the hall, memories of another place and another time flooded over me: the sights and sounds, the familiar smell of chalk, ink and dust assailed my senses. I saw again a schoolroom, filled with students in white shirts and navy-blue tunics, and I felt the pain of being there but not one of them. I saw again the skinny kid – a hybrid of two cultures and two colours – with bare feet and faded floral cotton dress, sitting in the front row and staring out of the classroom window, fantasising of one day being beautiful and famous.

Part One

1938

Paddington, Brisbane

Our house in Paddington was small and dark. The heavy curtains across the narrow sash windows were always drawn, and the windows closed. No light penetrated the gloomy interior. The front door led directly onto the street, with only one step down onto the footpath. There was a small verandah leading from the front door into a long dark hallway with bedrooms on either side, and finally through to the kitchen and the back door. Here there was a staircase of twelve or thirteen steps that descended to the backyard.

The front door was kept locked at all times. Our family and friends entered via the back gate, up the back stairs and sat in the kitchen. There wasn't anywhere else to sit.

The rest of the house was crammed with beds, including the front verandah, which was also enclosed and dark.

Eleven people were squeezed into this tiny old wooden

house. We lived there until I was seven. Mum, Dad and nine children. My half-brother Robert, the eldest, was working away from home. I seem to recall that he was working on Kenilworth station then. The youngest was baby Mary, who was born in 1941. Her nickname was Alice and mine was Freddie – lots of us had nicknames.

So we were living there in Paddington when my formal education began at the Milton State School in Brisbane, Queensland. My first memory, at age four, is vividly real and terrifying – a forerunner of what was to be my experience of life. It was my first day of school and I was being dragged along the road – crying hysterically – by my older sister Beryl.

I don't remember actually being at school then, or for some years later. It's possible my school experience was either so bad that I have blocked it from my consciousness, or so unremarkable as to be forgettable.

∞

My father had an innate fear of anyone knowing his business. Although it is everybody's right to protect his or her privacy, his fear went beyond that. It was almost a phobia. That was why our house was so dark. We weren't allowed to open the windows or draw back the curtains, for fear someone might see in. He drummed into us from birth, 'If anybody asks you any of our business, you say, I don't know.'

I never liked that house. Apart from the darkness and the secrecy, bad things happened there. Like the time my brother John was trying to dig a garden in the backyard to plant some small tomato plants he'd found at the dump.

John was only nine years old and he was having trouble lifting the garden pick. He had dug a patch about two feet square, when a little black and white puppy, belonging to my older brother Rod, jumped into the garden just as the pick was descending.

John didn't see the puppy – not until he raised the pick again and saw the little body impaled on the metal spike.

It was a terrible thing for all of us to see, but mostly for John. As Dad retrieved the puppy's body and took it away to bury it, John sat on the steps and bawled his head off. He was so softhearted he wouldn't deliberately hurt anything, and to kill a puppy like that almost broke his heart.

∞

It was always a relief to get out of the house. Mum sent me to the butcher shop on the corner to get the meat. Our icebox was a wooden chest with two doors. But the top half – a metal compartment for a block of ice, which kept the food cold in the lower compartment – was leaking and food wouldn't keep more than a day. It was my job to buy the meat for our dinner every day. The meat order was always the same so I didn't need a note, but Mum had given me some silver coins in a tin about two inches long, an inch wide and an inch deep. It normally held Vesta wax matches but, now empty, it served as a convenient way to carry money.

This day the butcher made fun of me, saying in a loud sing-song voice as I entered the shop, 'I know what you want, sixpence worth of stewing steak and a penny beef bone.' Then he guffawed loudly, with the waiting customers joining in.

I didn't really understand what the joke was, but I knew they were laughing at me. I was mortified. When the butcher turned his back, I left the shop and ran as fast as I could for home.

As I ran into the kitchen I burst into tears and told Mum what had happened. She was angry with the butcher and said, 'It's not bad enough that people like us have to be so poor, but smart alecs like him have to make fun of us.'

Then Mum asked, 'Where's the meat?'

'I didn't get it,' I replied tearfully.

Mum was angry with me. 'You stupid child, go straight back and get that meat. Your father will be home in a minute and I haven't even started the dinner.'

As an afterthought she added, 'Don't take any notice of that butcher, just get the meat . . . Oh yes, and Freddie, you had better get half a pound of tomatoes too, for lunches tomorrow.' She dropped more coins into the tin box.

Just then John came in the back door.

'John,' Mum said, 'go up to the shops with Freddie. You go and pick up the meat while she gets some tomatoes from the fruitshop. And hurry, it will be dark soon.'

'Okay,' John said. 'Come on, Freddie.'

He took me by the hand and pulled me along to make me keep up with his great strides. John was tall for his age and his long legs covered a lot more of the bitumen road than my short legs could.

When I left the greengrocer's with the tomatoes, the butcher shop was closed and John was nowhere to be seen.

Thinking he had gone on ahead of me, I ran to catch up with him, the change rattling loudly in the tin box.

As I turned into King Street, John was still nowhere in sight. I could see our house a long way down near the bottom of the hill, the electric light shining in the window of our kitchen, the rest of the house in darkness. As I slowed to a walk I felt the chill of the night air through my thin dress and realised it was getting dark.

Suddenly, a figure loomed up in front of me.

For a moment I thought it was John. But this person was a lot bigger than him.

∞

I don't remember much about what happened after that. I can only remember the man picking me up, and the sharp pain in my pee-hole that seared through my whole body.

I screamed and the man threw me to the ground and ran off.

Then I got up and started to run down the hill. Inexplicably the tomatoes were rolling down the hill beside me and I was passing them. Now Mother and Father had heard my screams and were running up the hill towards me. I was unaware of the warm blood coursing down my legs.

The man was never caught and my parents never spoke of this attack again.

1942

When Australia was threatened by Japanese invasion, my father bought an old truck and loaded up furniture, family and possessions, and we headed for the relative safety of the Queensland outback.

People were very frightened in those days. The Japanese had bombed Hook Island and Darwin in the Northern Territory, and Townsville in northern Queensland, and were reported to be marching down through the Cape York Peninsula. Because of the immense size of Queensland, the government didn't have the resources to defend the whole eastern seaboard of Australia. Most of our troops were overseas defending Britain, so the decision was made to form a line of defence on the south bank of the Brisbane River, codenamed 'The Brisbane Line'.

As my family lived in Paddington on the northern side of the river, it was a wise move to go bush.

Mitchell, central Queensland
Nine years old

It was winter and bitterly cold when we arrived in Mitchell. The only place we could find to live in was a broken-down house about a mile out of town. Following the river, the road surface became loose and sandy and our heavily laden truck found it hard going. When we finally arrived we saw a huge pepperina tree growing in the front yard. It looked a lot like a weeping willow, with its tiny leaves on long willowy fronds that almost touched the ground.

We were all tired and thirsty, but although there was running water in the taps, we couldn't drink it because of the foul smell and taste. Dad said it was bore water pumped up from the ground. He managed to find a galvanised-iron water tank, raised up off the ground on little, round, amputated wooden stumps. After much tapping with his knuckles up and down the side of the tank, Dad announced the tank was about three-quarters full. Then he turned on the tap and tasted the water, shook his head and smelt and tasted it again.

After he had quenched his thirst, he laughed. 'It's sweet, clean rainwater!'

The building was a wooden frame house in such neglected condition it was dangerous. The walls and floorboards were rotten and we had to step carefully around the bad parts to save ourselves from going through the floor. All the windowpanes were broken, so Dad and the boys covered them with brown paper, gluing it on with a paste Mum and us girls made out of flour and water.

This makeshift windowpane managed to keep out the bitterly cold wind that whistled through the house, but it also kept out the sunlight and made the interior dark and gloomy. Little better than the Paddington house we had just left, I thought.

∞

The only bed we'd been able to fit on the truck was Mum's iron bed with the porcelain and brass decoration. So us kids slept in old wire-spring beds that were in the house when we came. The first night was fraught with crying children, and our sleepless parents were unable to determine what was wrong with us.

In the morning it all became too clear: our sheets were spattered with blood. We had been eaten alive all night by bed bugs. They were about the size of a small ladybird and had been living in the top and foot of the bed where the wire wrapped around a solid piece of wood that held it in place. Tossing and turning in our sleep, we'd squashed them into our sheets.

An unpleasant odour came from these blood-bloated bugs, which intensified when they were squashed. After that first night Dad poured boiling water along the top and bottom of the wire every evening at sundown to kill them. But it also caused the bugs to give off that disgusting odour, which has stayed with me all my life.

∞

We settled down to living in the bush and I loved it. I had a rather special, spiritual connection that was hard to explain. It was like all the trees and animals were my friends and I felt welcome.

My family wasn't prepared, though, for the bitter winter cold of Mitchell, where the temperatures often dropped below zero. Each morning the ground was covered in inches of thick white frost, clothes were stiff on the clothesline and the water was frozen in the taps. Our house was almost on the riverbank, but the Maranoa River that ran through the town was dry for most of the year and held water only in the rainy season. Mum just used the bore water for bathing and laundry washing, and at the time we relied heavily on the water tank. So when the taps froze up, mostly only the babies were bathed because of the shortage of water.

Still, the rainwater in the tank got very low. And as the seasons changed from autumn and winter to spring, the temperatures rose accordingly. Soon there was a distinct odour and funny taste in the water.

Rod was sent to investigate and he found dead frogs in the tank. They'd probably been there when we moved in and had died when the water temperature fell too low. The extreme cold had also preserved their bodies, so they didn't rot until the water warmed up.

When Dad told Rod to get the frogs out with a rake, Rod said, 'I can't, they're rotten and falling apart.'

This made us all feel very sick and I can barely write about it today without experiencing that same nauseous feeling I had then. However, health-wise, the frogs did not harm us and we survived the change of seasons with no more than the common cold. But not so the summer. As temperatures soared above the century mark we were attacked by swarms of disease-carrying mosquitoes. Then, at the height of summer, the whole family came down with the dreaded dengue fever.

People often die from this disease, which causes extremely high temperatures and fever. Because we were all stricken at once, the town council believed the mosquitoes responsible were, ironically, breeding in our water tank, and they treated it accordingly.

I remember very little about this time. I can only recall being very sick and my mother standing beside me placing cool rags on my forehead. I can see her tortured face above me, drenched in perspiration, as she tried to tend her sick children when she herself was fighting the disease.

∞

Because I was an ugly, buck-toothed child with a constantly running nose, or perhaps because of my black mother and the fact that we were forced to live in a dilapidated old house on the outskirts of town, teachers and students alike shunned me. My teacher at the Mitchell State School was a tall, gaunt, middle-aged, middle-class English woman. Her grey hair, which was severely drawn back into a tight bun, matched her tight, lipless mouth and hooded, deep-set, light tawny eyes, and gave her an insidious, reptilian look. She would gaze down at me, along her long thin nose with narrow pinched nostrils, and when she spoke, you could see her small, even, square teeth.

I hated her. But worse, I was frightened of her.

It wasn't only me she despised. She hated Aboriginals and migrant kids – anyone, in fact, who was different. God help you if you had a speech impediment: that teacher had the kids hysterical with laughter as she walked with a mincing step while mimicking tortured speech.

But it was the blacks that copped the worst treatment. Mostly she ignored them, but when she spoke of them at all, it was to refer to them as 'those dirty uncivilised creatures'.

The classroom was divided down the middle, with desks on either side. And the teacher's desk was right at the centre front of the classroom. The long wooden desks had grey ceramic inkwells and a shallow, hollowed-out horizontal section in which to rest your pen and pencils. Those desks had innumerable initials and names of past and present pupils carved into them.

Behind each desk, as many as five or six pupils sat together on one long wooden bench. These were hard and uncomfortable, as were the bare wooden floorboards of the classrooms. The school building was made of wood and had galvanised-iron roofs that made the rooms unbearably hot. Most days in the summer it was so hot your pants were soaked with perspiration and your bare legs stuck to the seat. Often the windows had to be shut to keep out the fine red dust that blew in and swirled around the room, finally settling and coating everything in red powder. When the air was still and the windows were opened again, a loud buzzing sound announced the arrival of hordes of flies (fresh from the dung heap) to slake their thirst in the corners of our eyes.

The student who was 'top' of the class – the one with the highest marks – was seated in the back row on the extreme right of the room. Second top sat next to her, and so on until it came to the front three rows, where the blacks, the Chinese kids and the dunces sat. This was also where I spent most of my school days.

Aboriginal hybrid

At the height of the baby boomer phenomenon, that period during and following World War II when there was an explosion in the number of babies being born, white people were still very afraid of black people. Some openly showed their disgust by shrinking away from you. It was not easy, either, for a light-skinned Aboriginal person to pass as European. Although, by intermarriage with Europeans your skin may have turned white, your facial features still betrayed you. It was very hard for families, and particularly for children, to be an Aboriginal hybrid. Just as a child sometimes resembles one parent and not the other, so it is with the depth of colour in the skin. My brothers had Mum's dark skin (John was almost black) and broad features. The girls were a mixture of broad features and European features like my father. Nowadays there is a mix of ethnic people from all over the world with many different faces, but in Australia in the 1930s people were predominantly Anglo-Saxon, with fine, chiselled features and the peaches-and-cream complexion of the English rose. Compared with those delicate English, Irish and Scottish features, my broad, fleshy nose with wide flaring nostrils, heavy overhanging brows, and broad receding forehead, identified me as an Aboriginal.

Today, when I tell people I'm of Aboriginal descent, they are surprised and exclaim, 'But you are white!' There is never any mention of my features.

When I was a girl, the Australian people were still xenophobic, too, about the Asian races, who were known colloquially as 'The Yellow Peril'. Charles Darwin's theory of evolution remained very much in the forefront of people's minds. His 'Tree of Life' was a scale of the living species, on which he placed the white European races at the highest point. About halfway down the tree were the Asian races. Nearer the bottom were the black races, just above the apes. From this, people concluded that the black races were a subhuman species.

In this schoolroom, the teacher rarely spoke to or even acknowledged the presence of the pupils in the front rows. People have asked me many times why, if the teacher wanted to ignore us, we were seated closest to her. Of course the answer is simple: she was able to look over the top of us if we were in the front and pretend we weren't even there. The only time she ever spoke to the front-row pupils, including me, was to remind us of how stupid we were, and how mankind would benefit if we all blew away in the next big wind. She certainly didn't recognise the creative person within me, just waiting to emerge.

The Yumba

There was an Aboriginal camp on the other side of the Maranoa River, known as the Yumba. One night we could hear singing and a strange throbbing sound interspersed with shrill animal noises. Mum told us it was a musical instrument called a didgeridoo.

'A what zoo?' we cried, not having heard this word before.

Before she could explain, Dad came in saying, 'Well, that's bloody lovely, how long are those boongs going to keep that racket up?'

Mum didn't answer. She silently went back into the kitchen. However, the sound of singing and the hypnotic throb of the music were like a magnet to my brother Rod. Even though Mum had told us all to keep away from the Yumba, the next day Rod went to investigate.

But he had only just climbed out of the riverbed when five or six naked young blackfellas, who had been watching Rod, rose up out of the long grass. They were armed with long sticks sharpened at one end and, with a chilling war whoop, they came at him at full speed.

Rod ran for his life over the top of the dried bindies and burrs, his bare feet hardly touching the ground. When he reached home the back door was closed, so he dived under the house.

Now, the house was barely eighteen inches off the ground and there was very little room to manoeuvre. Mum, alarmed at the noise of Rod screaming, burst through the back door only to be confronted by the armed blackfellas.

Mum raised her fist in the air. 'What are you kids doing here? Go on, get going before I belt the lot of you.'

'But missus, we was only having a bit of fun, we didn't mean nothin',' the tallest one said.

'But you frightened my boy almost to death,' she said angrily.

'He not screaming 'cause of us,' another one said. 'There's a wild cat ripping inta him and he can't get out.'

Then two of the biggest boys went under the house and dragged Rod out by the feet.

This was our first meeting with the local Aboriginals. But we were never able to be friends with them. They didn't like anyone near the camp, and we were forbidden to visit it.

1944

Charleville, Queensland, aged 10
The angel

After a year in Mitchell we moved to Charleville. Life was better there; we lived in a flat closer to the town.

Each evening just before sunset, a whole herd of goats walked down the street and passed our flat. We were fascinated. The ladies were called 'nanny goats' and the boys were called 'billy goats'. The young goats were called 'kids'. They were of many colours, including pure white, black and white, brown, and brown and white, and all different colours in between. After school we would coax the biggest and strongest billy goat into our yard and ride him bareback. But how cranky some of those goats were! They would run under the lantana bush that grew in our front yard, or rub against the corner of the house trying to dislodge us. In the end the pain of our cuts and bruises took the fun out of it and we lost interest in riding the goats.

Soon after this, though, Dad brought home two beautiful white kid goats for us to feed and take care of. I wanted to take them to bed with me, but Dad said they had to sleep in the shed at night. I loved those baby goats, and the little bells – like pendulums – that hung from their necks fascinated me. I would go out every day and collect fresh green grass for them to eat.

Early one morning I woke up to hear the little kid goats crying out loud as if they were frightened. Thinking a dingo was attacking them, I rushed to their aid – just in time to see Dad cut their throats.

The two kids were strung up in the air by their feet.

I stood there paralysed with horror, and mesmerised by the blood gushing from their throats, forming a foaming pool on the ground.

When the cooked goat meat appeared on our table, I was sick and refused to eat it. I have never eaten goat meat since that day.

∞

At weekends, when other children were laughing and playing together, I would make my way to the Charleville Cemetery. I must have looked a lonely and forsaken child in the graveyard. But there nobody pushed me over or called me names. No, in the graveyard I felt at peace. I talked incessantly to myself, as I busily went on my rounds of the cemetery. I didn't think there was anything wrong with talking to myself, my father did it all the time, and he called it 'thinking aloud'.

My family never knew I played there. It was my secret place. That is, until one night when the river, swollen and angry, swept away my most prized possession.

The stone angel was about five or six inches high. She was dressed in a long gown with one tiny bare foot protruding beneath the hem. Her wings were partly folded, her hands outstretched, white, and quite weathered. Long exposure to the elements was evidenced by her smooth fingertips, which were worn down, almost to the first joint on each hand. Still I loved her. From the first time I saw the angel, standing at the base of a headstone by a small, untended grave, I wanted to have her. The grave was that of a child; though the inscription was eroded and difficult to read, I made out the name *Emilie*.

My play often took the role of housekeeping. I would straighten up overturned vases, throw away the dead flowers, and replace them with wildflowers or, if none were available, wattle-flowers from the acacia trees. Sometimes, I weeded the overgrown gravesites where nobody came to visit any more. I would always read the inscriptions on newly erected headstones.

The caretaker of the cemetery was a painfully thin, very tall, old man. I reckoned he must have been at least fifty, if not more. He always wore an old grey shirt and grey trousers, with braces to hold them up. His face was almost hidden by an old hat, pulled low over his eyes to protect him from the fierce glare of the sun. I was never close enough to see any detail in his face. But there was a rolled cigarette hanging from his bottom lip, seeming to defy gravity as it bobbed up and down when he spoke.

At first he used to chase me away. 'Get out of here,' he would say in a thick grave voice, interspersed with a chronic cough. 'This is no place for kids,' and 'Haven't you got a home to go to, girlie?' he would ask.

I never answered him.

Should anyone intrude into my world, the magic spell of the graveyard would be broken. So whenever the old caretaker approached, I would run down to the furthermost corner of the graveyard, to the wooden fence that surrounded the cemetery. In this corner, the fence had two loose palings, which I pushed aside far enough to slip through. Once outside I would wait in the scrub until he was out of sight, then I would return.

Later, he stopped chasing me and just ignored me.

I was returning from one of my flights through the back fence when I noticed her. It was a bleak, cold, overcast day when I took the angel. At the time, I fully intended to return her, but the angel was so much nicer to play with than sticks and 'Dolly' pegs that I wanted to keep her for a while.

I spent many happy hours with my angel, always placing her safely in the hollow trunk of a tree in the dry bed of the Warrego River.

Then, one night when the town and I were sleeping, nature unleashed a flood of rain. What had been a dry riverbed suddenly became a raging torrent.

It was several weeks before I was able to reach the tree where I had hidden the angel. But when the water subsided, I discovered she was gone. My angel had been washed away by the floods. I was devastated. Not only because I couldn't play with her any more, but also – I couldn't put her back.

1944

Leaving Charleville, aged 10

Not long after the flood took the angel, my family moved back to Brisbane. It would be thirty years before I returned to Charleville and the graveyard.

With the old truck loaded up with furniture, Mum, kids and bedding, we made the long, hazardous journey back. On the way we made frequent stops – not rest stops: Dad was either pulling off tyres or rolling about under the truck or, most often, hanging half in and half out of the engine. He was extremely bad-tempered, cursing and swearing at the truck, the tools, at Mum and the boys. At these times, we made ourselves as scarce as possible, keeping out of sight and out of range of flying objects.

At one creek the crossing was so steep and narrow, Dad had to unload the truck, and he and my three older brothers carried the furniture across piece by piece. Then he carried the children across. I knew he could do anything so I wasn't afraid, and I sat proudly on his shoulders as he traversed the deep running creek. Mum waded across with baby Mary. Then we all watched fearfully. Dad got in the truck and slowly drove down into the creek, but before the rear wheels of the truck had reached the water, the front wheels were climbing up the opposite bank. Time after time as he tried to make the truck climb out of the creek it slipped back into the water.

Eventually the engine boiled.

Dad got out, saying, 'I'll have to let her cool down a bit and have another go at getting her out later. In the meantime, you kids scout around, find some branches, and for Christ's sake don't pick up any bloody snakes!' He said this with great emphasis.

'Come on, you boys,' Dad said then, 'grab an axe, and we'll cut some saplings to make a ramp, it'll give the tyres more to grip on.'

By this time the sun was going. As it slipped below the horizon, the encroaching darkness began to overtake the long purple shadows on the ground. Without warning, we were attacked by swarms of bloodthirsty mosquitoes. These pests are always in the bush, day and night, but at dusk they attack ferociously. Mum rushed to pick up all kinds of animal dung – cow, horse, sheep and kangaroo – it all served the same purpose, though cowpats lasted the longest. She told us kids to stay put while she searched – there was too much danger of getting lost in the dark, especially in unfamiliar country.

Mum collected the dung in her skirt, and then piled it up high and set it alight. Dung doesn't burn as wood does, rather it smoulders like sawdust, giving off huge clouds of smoke. This billowed high into the trees, driving away all of the mosquitoes. The smell was atrocious and we ran to escape the smoke and the choking stench. Then we ran back into the smoke to escape the mosquitoes that, having tasted blood, still hung around beyond the smoke.

Arriving back in Brisbane

Finally, after many more stops, we arrived in Brisbane. A dishevelled, bedraggled, travel-weary troupe, we pulled up outside Aunty Gladys and Uncle Tom's house. They lived on Brisbane's north side, not far from the Brisbane General Hospital.

Aunty Gladys was my mother's sister. She was kind to us, but I disliked her house very much: it had a smell that reminded me of a hospital. We were told later that Aunty Gladys was a diabetic and had to inject herself with insulin every day; this accounted for the antiseptic smell that wafted through her house.

But we weren't there for very long, maybe only a few weeks, when Uncle Tom did something that made Dad very angry.

I saw my father, then, in a way I had never seen him before.

Growling like an animal, he lunged at Tom and pounded his face to a pulp. It was frightening.

Long after it happened, I remember with horror the sickening crunch as bone hit bone. There was blood everywhere;

we were all crying and begging Dad to stop but he thrashed Tom unmercifully.

Just around the corner

We left that house the same day, and moved to Grandfather's, just around the corner.

Grandfather's house was an old wooden building, the white paint starting to show signs of wear here and there; but at a distance it looked neat and tidy.

From the gate, it was only about a metre to the front steps of the house. There were nine or ten steps, leading up to a lattice door.

Oddly, there was a rather pretentious bronze plaque attached to the right-hand side of the house, level with the top of the steps. Visitors to the house (though they were mainly bill collectors) could not help but notice the plaque, which read *Hazelwood*.

Once inside the small front porch, there was a large solid oak door with a brass knocker. In the middle of the door was an elaborately carved, solid wood doorknob.

Most houses of this type had a long hallway running in a straight line from the front door, through the kitchen, to the back door. Lounge and dining areas were towards the front of the house while bedrooms were right and left of the hallway. The houses of this design built around the 1920s and 1930s were situated so close to each other that people often remarked that they could shake hands with their next-door neighbour from the windows. One might think that living in such close proximity would be an invasion of privacy. But this was not the case. The thick weatherboard outer walls, together with wooden tongue-and-groove interior walls, gave sufficient soundproofing to ensure a family's privacy.

There were, however, the windows to consider: glass being poor insulation against noise, these were usually insulated from within with heavy velvet and damask curtains. In poorer homes like ours, heavy floral cotton cretonne, or simply heavy folds of unbleached calico, would provide a measure of soundproofing.

Only Father and Mother and the girls lived at home now: Beryl, aged sixteen; Helen, twelve; Esmae, nine; Jan, seven; Mary, three; and I was eleven. My older brother Robert had joined the army. He was in the Light Horse Brigade. He looked very smart in his leather leggings and with the emu feathers in his upturned army hat. Rod was fifteen, and the oldest of Mum and Dad's children. Next eldest was Patrick at fourteen, and John at thirteen. These three boys were all away working in the bush.

My grandfather, whose place it was, inexplicably lived in a tent under the house. He was a silversmith and made some wonderful pieces of silver jewellery. Mum told us he'd also made fancy-dress costumes for them when they were small. I have a photo of my mother wearing a headdress Grandfather made. He also wrote songs and poetry, some of which have survived. However, to me he was a strange, silent figure with snow-white hair and a long beard, and he had an unnerving habit of peering through the flap of the tent with one eye. I was always a little afraid of him but I don't know why. Helen liked him.

The American army base

Across the road from our street was the American army base camp. Each weekday at precisely 7.45 a.m. the American band marched up the road towards where we went to school. Every day, Esmae, Jan and I marched up the hill with the soldiers, sometimes carrying their musical instruments, on our way to school. We were the only kids to do this – the other kids' parents had forbidden them to have anything to do with the soldiers or the army camp.

Starting work

At eleven, I left school and went to work. I was exceedingly grateful to leave behind those brief but humiliating and unhappy school days where I'd spent six years sitting in the front row of the classroom while the smartest kids sat in the back. I used to wonder whether, if I won a lot of money in the Golden Casket (the old lottery), I would also become smart. There were no poor kids in the back row: if you were white you were rich and smart, if you were black you were dumb and poor.

Dad was happy for me to leave school. He believed education was wasted on girls. But, more importantly, he did not want to have to support us for too long.

When each one of us started work, Mum had to take us to a loan office, the Brisbane Credit Company, and take out a five-pound credit voucher for one of the large chain stores such as T.C. Beirne's or McDonnell and East. For us girls, this five-pound voucher would buy a black skirt, two white blouses, underwear, and a pair of shoes. Starting from our first pay packet we would pay Dad half our wages for room and board. My wages were about thirty shillings a week. I would give Dad fifteen shillings and pay five shillings to the Credit Company, then I would have ten shillings left to cover bus fares, clothes and entertainment.

Greek cafe

My first job was as a counter attendant at a milkbar in Fortitude Valley. A Greek who had a liking for little girls owned it. His wife was there most of the day but at night I was alone with him. I could barely see over the counter, so he put a fruit box there for me to stand on.

The first thing he told me was that I could eat as much ice-cream and lollies as I wanted. I thought he was a generous boss – but he knew if he told me not to eat the lollies I would sneak some anyway. After a couple of days of stuffing myself with treats and sweets I had no desire to touch any of the stock again.

I had to work very late at night in that job. The last bus came around eleven o'clock. But between the closing of the milkbar and the arrival of the bus, I had ten minutes to wait alone at the bus stop. I was very frightened, but I was also too frightened to stay in the shop with the Greek owner after it closed.

After that I had several milkbar jobs, leaving each one mainly because of sexual interference by the bosses. I worked in cafes, and later graduated to better-class restaurants as I gained experience.

But soon my working life would be interrupted.

I would be thrown from a horse before I had learned to ride properly, and receive a deep puncture wound in my right leg. This developed into an ulcer that took six months to heal. I was working in a very good restaurant when it happened, but I was put off because of the bandage on my leg. Unhygienic, they said, so I had to go.

1945

Twelve years old
'The Girl in the White Dress'

I was up early preparing for my Sunday walk. I wouldn't be starting out until mid-morning, but this was such an important occasion, careful preparations were made to ensure that the walk – perhaps it could be called a ritual walk – was both stimulating and satisfying.

My white socks and white sandshoes had been vigorously scrubbed and allowed to dry overnight. Sunday morning, my shoes were whitened with Kiwi paste. My white dress was carefully ironed by my mother who paid meticulous attention to the rows and rows of tiny lace on the puffed sleeves and the Peter Pan collar. From the throat to the waist there were small self-covered buttons arranged closely together and hooked through small loops of the same white fabric.

My straight brown hair was parted on the right side and tied back with a white ribbon.

When all was in readiness and I was in my white dress, shoes and socks, I set out on my walk.

'Bye, Mum,' I said as I left the house. But this wasn't what I really wanted to say. I couldn't find the words, not then anyway. Strange how easily words come after the event, when it is too late to say them.

∞

As I left the house, I looked back over my shoulder, intending to wave, but my mother had already gone back inside. Then I was aware that I had already turned the corner. I felt a little angry that an essential part of my walk had gone by without me realising it. Never mind, I thought, I know I look nice in my white dress, shoes and socks, and I won't be angry, because people can see when you are angry, and I won't look nice any more.

I knew from experience that when a person was cross their face became swollen and red and somehow got out of shape. Their voice became strangled and harsh and they coughed and spluttered and were truly ugly, even the pretty ones.

I didn't like to think too much when I went walking, I needed to observe the people I saw along the way. I had been taking this walk for several months now – in fact, ever since Vivien's mother (a neighbour who lived across the road) had given me the special white dress. It was the nicest dress I had ever owned. Up until then I had worn family clothes, sort of conjointly owned with my sisters, at least those who'd been about my size.

Perhaps because Vivien's mother had specifically said, 'Here is a dress for Audrey,' Mum had let me own it.

Now, as I walked slowly up the hill towards Ballymore football field, I paid particular attention to the windows of the houses I passed. It excited me when I saw either a face or a moving curtain at the window. It meant someone was watching me. My sisters would have been horrified to experience such strange public attention, but I loved it. I wanted people to notice me, I fantasised that people were secretly admiring my lovely white dress with its frilly Peter Pan collar and frilly puffed sleeves and my immaculate white socks and sandshoes.

Nobody ever knew where I went on my Sunday walks, and nobody cared enough to ask. I just travelled a huge circle, returning home tired and flushed, yet still immaculately white and clean.

Seven Hills

Around 1945 we moved to the pleasant Brisbane suburb of Seven Hills. Partly suburbia and partly rural, it was about fifteen miles from the city. Our house was a neat low-set weatherboard structure, painted a pale cream colour with a dark green trim, and a red-tiled roof. The three bedrooms were quite inadequate and the girls had to sleep four to a bed.

At the end of the street, just a short distance from our

house, there was a vast paddock dotted with huge shady gum trees; we dubbed this 'the bull paddock' due to the angry, lone black bull that lived there. We spent a great deal of time playing in this paddock, while we kept a wary eye out for the bull. That bull had long sharp horns and we were terrified he might charge us one day. But he never did. He just delighted in sneaking silently up behind us, then letting out the most nerve-shattering roar he could muster. Kids would scatter in all directions.

∞

All my life I had loved horses, and when we moved to Seven Hills I yearned to own my own horse. When I was earning I would often hire a horse from Mrs Kemp's riding school. She always gave me a horse called Splash, obviously so named because of his orange and white paint-splashed coat.

Undeterred by my previous accident, I learned to ride on Splash. He looked for the entire world like one of the American Red Indian paint ponies we saw in the Western movies. Splash was a docile horse who went at his own pace regardless of what the rider wanted. I soon found it was easier and much more enjoyable just to let Splash have his own way.

My mother

Winifred Anne May was a softly spoken gentle Aboriginal woman. She had soft brown eyes and dark brown wavy hair that framed her once lovely face. Her mother, my grandmother, came from the country of the Gunggari/Kunja language tribal groups in central Queensland. Nana's actual birthplace is not recorded but it is thought to be around Charleville. Her birthday is given as 1865. She married a white man.

My mother was born in 1903 in the garden of a house in a small country town called Stonehenge. Stonehenge is in central Queensland, about 300 miles from Longreach where I was born. Stonehenge had no hospital, not that it would have been any use to my grandmother as Aboriginal women were not permitted to give birth in hospital.

My mother grew up to become a comfortable fat lady who shook all over like jelly when she laughed. Being of the zodiac sign Sagittarius – a fire sign like me – my mother was a free spirit. It was a great tragedy and a sin against nature that she was burdened with the violent and oppressive bondage of her marriage.

By the time my mother was thirty-eight she had had eleven children. The last baby, a little girl, was stillborn. Her two eldest children, Beryl and Robert, had been born to another man, before her marriage to my father. My grandmother had raised them, until she died of pneumonia in 1933.

There were times, though, when the high-spirited, fun-loving fire sign would emerge in my mother. When a popular song came over the wireless, she would whirl around the kitchen, twirling the tea towel over her head like a gypsy dancer. Often, we kids would join in the fun. Mum would stretch the tea towel between her hands and, while she was still dancing, several of us would grab the middle of the cloth and jump up and down. At these times my mother's face would light up, there was laughter in her eyes and the years rolled away.

Sometimes, Dad would come in, angry at having his peace disturbed. 'What's all this racket about?' he would roar. Then, to us kids, 'Go on, get outside and play,' pushing us roughly towards the door.

I looked at my mother, but her face had shut down, her shoulders drooped, and a broken old woman stood in her place. Yet, despite her unhappiness, she was able to express herself in her poetry, her oil and watercolour paintings, and her music. Mum taught herself to play the piano by ear.

Arachnophobia

Apart from my mother's kind and gentle nature, I also remember vividly her fear of things that crawled. Of all the creepy crawlies, her greatest dread was spiders. I guess most people fear or simply dislike spiders, but my mother's fear bordered on arachnophobia. My brothers, being typical larrikins, thought it hilarious to leave huge lifelike shells of large spiders in the pantry or in the laundry basket. Some of these shells were as big as saucers. Not content with just planting these fearful creatures where Mum was sure to come across them, the boys experimented with bits of cotton tied to the legs of the spider shells to make them move. Sometimes they even attached the cotton to the cupboard door, causing the 'spiders' to spring out when the door was opened. Mum's hysterical screams would send the boys rolling on the ground in fits of laughter.

One day Rod and Patrick arrived home with a huge bunch of green bananas, the stem still moist from being freshly cut, and stood the bunch on the kitchen floor.

'Where did those bananas come from?' Mum asked suspiciously, tapping her foot as she waited for the boys to answer. My family was very strict when it came to stealing. Even the smallest crime would beget a severe belting with the razor strop.

'We didn't pinch them, Mum,' Patrick said defensively, 'we found them just like that, lying on the side of the road – didn't we, Rod?'

Rod, by now a tall, skinny kid with a long neck, nodded his head vigorously in agreement. Then he found his voice.

'Yes, they was just lying there on the side of the road with nobody owning them. So we just said, if nobody owns these bananas we might as well take them home before somebody else does!'

Mum could see the reasoning in this and decided to give them the benefit of the doubt. 'All right,' she said. 'But you can't eat them yet because they're green. I'll hang them in the pantry until they ripen.'

With that she grasped the end of the bunch and lifted. As she did so a huge spider came out of the bananas and ran up Mum's arm. Her screams could be heard half a mile away. The warmth of the kitchen fire had quickened the spider, which up until then had been snugly curled into a tight little ball safely wedged between the cool green bananas. Suddenly aware that its home had been invaded, it made a run for it. But the shrill sound that rent the air momentarily stopped the spider in its tracks and, visibly shaken, it fell rather than jumped to the floor. There, summoning up all its courage, the spider raised itself high on its long, hairy legs and balefully stood its ground.

It was by far the biggest and ugliest spider I had ever seen. 'As big as a saucer', some of the kids described it later. Its legs were coated in long silky grey hair, while the body, covered with big grey lumps like warts, appeared swollen and grotesque. For a moment Mum stood and stared her most feared nightmare in the face. Then, slowly and deliberately, she reached behind her and grabbed the straw broom. Raising it over her head, Mum brought the broom down on the back of the spider.

The unthinkable happened.

The spider broke up into hundreds of tiny pieces and ran in all directions across the kitchen floor. What had appeared to be warts on its back were in fact hundreds of little spiderlings.

Suddenly the kids – until now transfixed by fear – all screamed and ran for the open door. For once, the big oaken doorway was not wide enough for us all to get out at once. We were jammed together, blocking the only exit – Mum was locked in a room full of spiders and caught in the flight-or-fight syndrome.

Flight now being impossible, Mum's fear turned to anger, and she went on the attack, pumping the old tin fly-sprayer, killing every spiderling she could see.

At last the bunch of bananas was taken out and hung in the woodshed, and eventually they were all eaten.

Our food

Us kids were never allowed in the house except at mealtimes and to go to bed. Meals were taken in relays: the kids were fed first, and then the adults. As I recall, we were never hungry. Our food was plentiful, but monotonous. We always had porridge for breakfast, usually 'Breakfast Delight' made from semolina and mixed with milk and sugar. This was followed by a thick slice of toast spread with golden syrup or treacle. The delicious smell of bread being toasted in the morning wafted through the house, drawing sleep-laden children from their beds.

The baker with a horse-drawn cart delivered our bread daily. We made toast by impaling a thick slab of bread on a long three-pronged wire fork, and holding it over the glowing coals in our Kookaburra wood stove. Mum, Dad and the older children drank Bushells tea, but the younger ones drank water.

For lunch, we had sandwiches. Mum piled up a plate with thick slabs of buttered bread and put it in the centre of the table. Each child helped themselves to the bread and both melon and lemon jam or Golden Syrup.

Dinner was usually stew. On occasions Mum curried it, but it was still stew. The older children would help feed the younger ones, though often the little ones would insist on helping themselves, and this was encouraged. Soon the young ones were as adept at feeding themselves as the older children. We had dessert once a week, on a Sunday, and it was either bread-and-butter pudding, baked in the large roasting dish in the oven, or baked rice pudding.

Sunday was a special day in our house. Instead of having

our main meal in the evening around five o'clock, on Sunday we would have it at midday and it was Dad's turn to cook. In answer to our question, 'What are we having for pudding today, Pop?', Dad would smile in that special way and say, 'That's my secret and you will find out when I'm good and ready to tell you.' Dad loved secrets, you could tell by the way his blue eyes softened and crinkled at the corners how happy he was. Although his voice was gruff, we instinctively knew he was playing a game. After all, there were only two choices – either bread-and-butter pudding or baked rice pudding. But on odd occasions, Dad would cook a boiled fruitcake, which was served with a sweet white sauce. I never knew then why we didn't have the fruitcake more often. Now I realise it was more expensive to make than the puddings.

Jobs we had

My father didn't have any particular trade or training yet he was able to turn his hand to almost any manual-labouring job. When he worked for Hutton, Foggitt, Jones, a small goods company on Roma Street in the city, he used to drive a long cart, drawn by two draught horses. One day the horses took fright and bolted, toppling Dad from his tall seat onto the road. He landed under the cart – and two of the ironclad wheels passed over his legs. Fortunately the cart was empty; had it been fully laden Dad may have lost his legs.

My sister Beryl, who was seventeen, worked at Arnott's biscuit factory. The one thing I remember about this job was the large packet of broken biscuits she brought home for the family every week. Meanwhile, Helen, who was fourteen, worked at the Brisbane Bag and Paper Company, while I, at twelve, having been fired from the last job, worked at the rival paper-bag factory, Paper Products. My most vivid memory of this time is of the edge-to-edge, dusty pink, boxy jacket Helen wore to work. I was very envious of that jacket. But I was also very proud of Helen because she had knitted it herself.

My father a Goliath

My father was a very striking man. He had regular features and a strong, square jaw. His chin jutted aggressively, an indication of his determined and unforgiving nature. However, his most remarkable feature was his eyes. They were blue. Not just any blue, but a deep fluid colour that mirrored the thoughts and emotions of his heart and soul. The depth of blue in my father's eyes rose and fell like a wind-charged sea, making him the most readable person I have ever known. Perhaps that is why us kids were so well behaved. He could stop us dead in our tracks, and hold us suspended – frozen in time and space – with just one petrifying, cold look.

There were times when Dad's eyes seemed darker than usual, a sort of dark, inky blue, like when he held the razor strop a full arm's length above his head before bringing it crashing down upon our backs or legs. Yet, when he was trying to contain his pent-up anger, Dad's eyes appeared to be lit from within by a cold blue candle, the colour pulsating with an inner life before exploding in a shower of blue sparks as he vented his anger.

By way of contrast, though, my father's eyes could sometimes be soft and warm like blue velvet or a darkening evening sky. This was especially true when he tirelessly tended us in our sickbed. He was a wonderful nurse and doctor, often curing us with some old bush remedy or other, but mostly willing us to recover with the strength of his own conviction that illness was a state of mind, not a physical thing. And we never doubted, this giant of a man could not be wrong, and we would always fully recover. Even Rod, Patrick, John and Helen had recovered, in the Longreach hospital, after they all contracted scarlet fever in 1933.

My father was especially attractive to women. He was well over six feet tall and very powerfully built. He always walked straight and tall, reminding me of a military person, though he had never served in the armed forces. He never ambled or strolled; he marched, his long strong legs seeming to cover metres in every stride. Even in my father's last year there was no sign of stooping; at sixty-eight he walked with his head held high and looked the world squarely in the eye.

Apart from his broad shoulders and strong, muscular body, my father was also very handsome. He had smooth, straight, jet-black hair, and a slow, pleasant smile, which was heralded by a funny crinkling at the corners of his eyes and around his nose, a mannerism women often found attractive. He was the proverbial ladies' man, which my mother found intolerable. Apart from his liking for other women, he also liked to feel up little girls. For as long as I can remember, my father was sexually molesting me. It was a disgusting practice, which I found degrading and unbearable. I loved my father very much. I remember how I wanted him to put his strong arms around me as I sat on his knee. Just like I had seen other fathers do with their own little girls.

But my mother said I must never go near my father or let him touch me, because what he did was dirty and wrong.

∞

One incident has remained as a most vivid memory of my father. I was about six years old. My dad called me to him as I came in through the front door.

'Come here, Freddie,' he said, calling me by my nickname. 'Sit on the lounge with me.'

I was so happy I climbed up on his lap. But when he slid his hand inside my pants and started stroking my genitals, I suddenly remembered what my mother had told me.

'No!' I cried angrily, pushing his hand away. 'Mum said that's dirty.'

My father pushed me roughly from his lap, then he grabbed me by one arm, dragged me to my feet and slapped me hard on the bum. 'Get out of here, you little bitch. Go on, get out.'

He didn't have to tell me a second time – I was already running with my bum on fire and screaming at the top of my voice down the hallway to my bedroom. My mother's voice followed me: 'Serve you right, I told you not to go near him.'

The unholy row that followed between Mum and Dad made me feel guilty, because I was the cause of it. Mum ended up with a black eye, and Dad stormed out and didn't return for two days.

∞

My father had many sides to his character. Just as he could reduce me to a mere object of lust, he could also be extremely cruel. He was an alcoholic and a violent man who constantly lashed out at my mother with his fists and sarcastic tongue.

My mother never drank alcohol and never went to the pub with Dad. I couldn't understand why they married. They had so little in common. My father was debonair, moderately educated and a racist. He hated the blacks, the Communists, the Nazis, the Jews, and all Asians – in fact, anyone who wasn't a white Australian of Irish and Cornish descent like himself. My father spent the rest of his life being ashamed of his wife and children because they were Aboriginal.

Dad often belittled us and Mum in front of other people. I didn't understand that he was embarrassed by us all. I often wondered why my mother and us kids always walked several steps behind him, in the rare times we were seen out in public together. For a while I thought that it was because my father had some sort of special standing in the community. Like royalty, where the Queen always walked a few steps behind the King as a mark of respect. However, it didn't take me too long to work it out: he was not only ashamed of our Aboriginality, he also had the audacity to feel ashamed because we were so many. 'Don't tell people I've got a mob of ten kids,' he would often say angrily, 'eight is all I've got.

The other two [Beryl and Robert] are your mother's, not mine.'

∞

If only Dad could have seen himself when he was drunk and violent and known how afraid and ashamed we were of him. Like the times when he was fighting with Mum and threatened to split her face open with an axe. How she fled the house in terror, and we went with her and crouched and huddled together behind the roosting chooks.

Mum held a finger to her lips and whispered, 'Hush, not a sound.'

I remember this as some sort of horrific nightmare. Our bare feet covered in chook manure, the fumes choking us, and not being able to slap the mosquitoes that bit ferociously and siphoned off our blood. 'Only female mosquitoes suck blood,' I recall Mum once said. And there were only terrified females hiding in the chook pen, behind the roosting hens.

We watched my father, out of his head with drink and armed with the wood-axe, swearing and cursing as he searched for Mum.

The concert

And there were other times when we were embarrassed by him.

He would land home drunk with a few old cronies, which often included women, and demand that his daughters display their talents in an impromptu concert they dare not refuse.

First on call would be my older sister Helen, who had a beautiful soprano voice. She would sing Dad's favourite, 'Danny Boy', with Mum accompanying her on the piano. Although Mum couldn't read a note of music, she could play any song if you just hummed a few bars for her. Next came my younger sister Jan. She was talented. She could dance and sing a Jane Powell routine almost as well as Jane herself. My sisters hated these sessions, but to refuse would get Dad's Irish up and make those steely eyes spark.

Perish the thought! It was easier to perform and get it over with.

Strangely enough, I was a willing and natural performer and I pleaded with my father to let me recite poetry, some of which I had written myself, or from the works of Henry Lawson and Banjo Paterson – 'The Outlaw of Glenidle' and 'The Man from Ironbark' – which I had memorised. But this was not my father's idea of entertainment and he got angry with me when I asked to have a turn.

'No, Freddie, don't be silly, you can't do anything. Go on, get out of the way.' Disappointed, I would go outside, sit on the back steps, nurse my old grey tomcat and cry, unable to understand why poetry wasn't as good as singing and dancing. But one night as I sat on the steps I suddenly noticed how the chooks all roosting on their perches reminded me of people sitting in a theatre.

Here, I thought, was my audience.

And from then on I would happily sit on the back steps

and recite poetry and sing sad songs, like 'Old Shep' and 'There's a Bridle Hanging on the Wall'. Songs so sad the tears would roll down my face and fall upon the cat's back.

Friday is bath day

My father was obsessed with washing his hands. He would ritually clean them for no apparent reason other than to roll a cigarette. And he never neglected to wash his face, neck and ears in cold water every morning, something the rest of the family were loath to do.

His weekly bath also had the appearance of a ritual, taking just on an hour to complete. It took gallons of hot water to fill the old grey galvanised bathtub which was supported on four large bird-like feet, each set of talons gripping a round metal ball. It was an ugly contraption but we had never known anything else.

On Friday nights, in readiness for the horse races on Saturday, Dad used to dip himself in the bath water, then, with the Lifebuoy soap, lather himself thoroughly all over, dip again to rinse off, then repeat the process over again several times. Lifebuoy soap was an unpleasant pinkish-red colour, but worse than that it had a powerful odour. Dad used to say it had a clean smell. But to us kids it smelt suspiciously like an insecticide. Maybe it was – Dad used to claim it was strong enough to kill fleas on the dog. He would come out of that bath red raw and shiny as a new penny, or, as Mum used to say, 'brand spanking new' . . . anyway, he did look as if several layers of skin had been peeled off.

The wood stove

There was no such thing as a hot-water system: the water for the bathtub was boiled up in two large, four-gallon kerosene tins on top of the stove, with the cast-iron hot plates removed to increase the heat.

Our Kookaburra wood stove was never allowed to go out. It served to cook our food, and to keep it warm on the hot plates as well as in the oven. It heated our Mrs Potts's irons, to iron our clothes. We dried our clothes in front of the fire in wet weather and in winter it warmed our whole house.

We would often just sit and stare into the glowing embers: either to dream and plan for the future, or to recall memories, and laugh or cry in retrospect.

Sometimes, we just sat and let the soothing warmth and glow of the embers mesmerise and anaesthetise our jaded nerves. My mum was very wise in a lot of ways and more perceptive than my father ever knew. She used to say, 'If you pour your worries into the fire, they will return to you as ashes and trouble you no more.' She was right, we often disposed of our troubles that way before going to bed, and in the morning things weren't nearly so bad. Last thing at night Mum would put a large log in the stove, close the fire door tightly and shut off the dampers. This forced the fire to die down to a slow smoulder so there would still be live embers in the morning.

The rebellious one

I was known as the rebellious member of our family and, by now, although I was only thirteen, I knew that most of the friction between my father and myself stemmed from my loyalty to my mother. Even at this tender age, I was old enough to know that my father shouldn't be belting my mother the way he did – especially when she was so sick. Mum had high blood pressure and rheumatoid arthritis that was painful and almost crippled her hands.

Although I was very frightened of my father, when he lashed out at my mother I stood up to him and defiantly told him to leave her alone.

These fights usually generated from my father's attempt to degrade and humiliate my mother because she was an Aboriginal. One day Dad was punching my mother and she was crying and desperately trying to protect her face with her hands. I yelled at him to stop, but he was punching and shouting abuse at her and he didn't hear me. I could stand it no longer.

I jumped in front of my mother, and my father's fist caught me a glancing blow on the side of the head.

I wasn't hurt but I made out I was.

Holding my head in both hands, I rolled my eyes back and cried out loudly, 'Oh, my head, my head.'

It had the desired effect – the fight was over.

'You bloody stupid interfering little bitch,' Dad yelled at me, his eyes blazing. He was so angry and frustrated he was almost crying. 'Get out of here and mind your own bloody business. Get out, you hear me, bloody well get out.'

Without a word, I left the room. That night, lying in bed, I decided to run away from home.

Running away from home

The next day I hired my favourite horse, the one named Splash, from Mrs Kemp's riding stables, and rode north to Caboolture, about thirty miles from Brisbane. As I rode, I thought about what I could do to support myself. At thirteen, I really didn't have many choices. I had mainly worked in milkbars owned by sleazy Greeks who liked feeling up little girls. I didn't want to return to that life. Instead I thought I really would like to work on a farm, caring for animals, and maybe even have my own horse.

∞

The trip up the Bruce Highway was pleasant and uneventful. That is, until I rode up the main street of Caboolture that evening. A uniformed policeman stepped in front of Splash. Taking hold of the bridle, he said gruffly, 'Are you Audrey May?'

'Yes,' I replied, frightened, my voice barely above a whisper.

'This horse has been reported stolen,' the policeman said, 'and your father has reported you missing. I think you had better turn around and go straight back home.'

But I was tired, aching and bone weary from having ridden so far – all I wanted to do was to lie down somewhere and go to sleep. I couldn't face the thirty-mile ride back home again.

So I asked the policeman if I could leave Splash in the police paddock for the night. He agreed.

Taking the bridle and saddle with me, I boarded the southbound train and returned to Brisbane.

∞

When I got home my father was very angry with me. Not only for running away, but because I had left the horse behind.

'Can't you do anything right?' he yelled, lashing me several times across the back with the razor strop. 'Now go back and get the bloody horse.'

The next morning I caught the early bus into the city, and boarded the train to Caboolture at Roma Street railway station. I took only the bridle, intending to ride home bareback. But this time it would take twice as long to get home.

After only a few miles riding without a saddle, my bum was red raw. I got off and walked, leading Splash behind me. Not that walking was much better than riding; either way I was in a lot of pain.

Finally, when it began to get late and the sun was setting, I realised I was too tired and too sore to go on any longer. So I looked for somewhere to spend the night.

The day before, as I'd passed that way heading north, I had noticed many farming properties, most of them with big tin sheds that were deserted and isolated from the homestead. A place to camp for the night, I thought, better than sleeping beside the road.

The night was clear and moonlit as I left the road and followed a narrow animal track along the fence. I guess I walked about half a mile before I found a paddock with a gate that I could lead Splash through. The shed was a large galvanised structure, though very old and unkempt. As I approached, the rusty old building seemed to sway slightly – no doubt this was an illusion of the flickering moonlight as thin clouds scudded across the sky. Inside, the place seemed even larger. It was packed with bales of hay loaded on top of each other, reaching almost to the roof. This, I knew, was winter feed for the cattle, sheep and horses, when green feed was scarce. Mrs Kemp had a shed like this, I thought, though not nearly so big. Hers was near empty most of the time.

I didn't have to tie Splash up: he began eating, and didn't intend to leave such a feast. As I lay down on the warm, sweet-smelling bales, I thought how much nicer the hay was than the four sweaty bodies in my bed back home. I closed my eyes and my last thought before sleeping was how furious Dad would be when I didn't come home that night.

Splash was still eating when I woke up the following morning.

∞

Yes. My father was angry, very angry, when I arrived home the next day. He got out the razor strop again and belted me across the back, legs and bum, saying over and over, 'When I tell you to come straight home, you do as you are told, you hear, you hear?'

Finally, his anger spent, he shoved me into the bedroom.

At times like these (and they were becoming increasingly frequent) I would sneak out of the house and go to my favourite swimming hole, the blue metal quarry at Morningside. It was several miles away, but as always I took a shortcut through the bull paddock. There I would swim, cooling my aching body, and try to quell the anger that boiled up inside me. Then, when it started to get dark, I made my way home and slipped quietly back into the house.

∞

The next day my father called me into the kitchen where he and Mum were sitting at the table drinking tea.

'You have to take that horse back this morning,' he said.

'Oh,' I wailed, 'I'm too sore, can't someone else do it?' I knew this was a stupid thing to ask because no one else in the family could ride, and they certainly wouldn't walk the two miles down and two miles back again.

'No,' Dad said, raising his voice. 'Mrs Kemp wants *you* to take the horse back. You are the one who took it in the first place so it's *your* responsibility to return it. Besides,' Dad said more quietly, 'Mrs Kemp wants to have a talk with you.'

I bet she does, I thought miserably, the only time anyone wants to talk to me is when I'm in trouble.

Still muttering to myself, I went to the back door. My heart lifted when I saw Splash quietly dozing in the sun. He was a funny-looking horse. Apart from his orange and white paint-splashed coat, he also had odd-coloured eyes, one brown eye and one blue eye that was partly covered with a thick thatch of white hair. He also had long white hair overlapping his hooves, like a draught horse.

At that moment, Splash looked more comical than ever. He appeared to be asleep, his head hanging low to the ground, one hind leg bent with the tip of the hoof resting on the ground. He looked as if he had broken something and was dying on his feet. Perhaps that was why I loved him so much. We were two of a kind: he was comical, and I was ugly. We didn't fit in and we belonged together, Splash and me.

I picked up the saddle and bridle from the rail on the back landing and, because my feet were sore from so much walking the day before, I stepped gingerly across the hard and stony ground. Apart from a mango tree that Dad had planted in the left-hand corner of the backyard, bindies and burrs were the only other plant life that grew in our yard.

The only time the yard was watered was in hot, dry, dusty conditions when Mum wanted to wash. Then Dad would go out and sprinkle water onto the ground with the hose, to lay the dust. Sometimes he would let us kids do it, but we usually turned the ground into a muddy quagmire, so Dad preferred to do it himself.

As I approached, Splash lifted his head and whinnied softly in greeting. He gently nuzzled my neck with his soft velvety nose, then stroked his chin across my shoulder. It felt nice. Our eyes met and I wondered if he knew this was to be our last ride together. Maybe he did. Anyway, I didn't have the heart to tell him. Instead, I looked up at him with a smile and said, 'Well, old fellow, it's time to take you home.' At the command 'Stand up', Splash obediently lowered his head for me to place the bit in his mouth and the bridle over his head. Mrs Kemp had told me that command, the first time I went there to hire a horse. The command 'Stand up', she said, when spoken in an authoritative voice, let the horses know they were now working.

When all was ready, I prepared for the difficult task of getting myself into the saddle. Mum told me that this kind of chafe was only superficial and would heal quickly if I didn't hurt it any more. So she put a generous handful of cornflour on the raw place on my bum and covered the injury with a small square piece of sheet, fastening the corners with plaster. Mum always had bits of old torn sheets that she kept clean and ready in a pillowcase for such emergencies. 'It probably won't stop it from hurting,' she said sadly, 'but at least it will stop further chafing if the skin doesn't rub together.'

Once in the saddle I shoved a doll's pillow (belonging to my sister Esmae) between my bum and the saddle and, although it still hurt a lot, this helped to soften the impact against the hard leather.

I let Splash amble along at his own pace and just enjoyed the closeness and companionship of my good friend. I always talked to Splash a lot on our rides together, and I am sure he enjoyed listening to my voice.

Finally we were there and Splash turned into the open gates of the riding stables. He knew what to do, he walked along the wooden rails of the yard to the tack shed and stopped outside and waited for me to dismount. There was nobody there to take care of Splash so I unsaddled him, rubbed him down with a coarse sack, then turned him loose in the grazing paddock.

Mrs Kemp

I looked up at the house and saw Mrs Kemp at a window watching me. I forced my feet to walk towards her, and as I went up the front steps I counted every one. There were thirteen, and at the top stood Mrs Kemp. I kept my gaze lowered until I saw her riding boots, then I stopped and slowly raised my eyes, up past the tops of her boots and trousers, past the plaid shirt to her chin, which, from where I was standing, looked to be resting on her bust.

Mrs Kemp always wore a man's shirt and trousers. She was a tall, imposing woman, powerfully built with large muscles and sinewy arms; except for her bust, she could have been a man. Since I'd first begun hiring horses from her, about a year earlier, Mrs Kemp had barely said more than a few words to me, and then only to growl 'Those stirrups are too long', or 'Tighten the girth strap, do you want to end up under his belly?' Her tanned leathery skin showed her love of the outdoors, yet she never seemed to be happy. She rarely spoke or smiled at anyone.

How I wanted to turn and run, and it took a huge effort to force myself to stand still. After all, I reasoned, the worst she could do was roar at me. She couldn't shoot me, could she?

'Come in, come in, child. Don't just stand there, the tea is getting cold,' said Mrs Kemp, a little impatiently.

I looked into her face then and saw just the hint of a smile.

Mrs Kemp led the way down a long hall towards the back of the house and into the kitchen. I saw the table was set for two on a fine linen tablecloth with the most beautiful china tea set I had ever seen. I was fascinated by the faces of lovely Chinese ladies painted on the inside of the cups.

'Help yourself to the scones,' Mrs Kemp said as she poured the tea.

I dragged my eyes away from the Oriental face in the bottom of the cup and saw the scones, still steaming from the oven. There were tiny glass dishes each with a teaspoon of jam or honey and a larger one with whipped cream. I looked around. There were horses everywhere. Horses in pictures on the wall, horse statues, and heads of horses – all over the room.

'You like horses very much, don't you?' Mrs Kemp asked, looking at me intently.

'Yes,' I replied simply.

While we ate the scones (they were light, fluffy and delicious) Mrs Kemp told me about the horses in the pictures. They were all show horses which had won many ribbons and prizes. But soon I lost interest: I didn't want to ride a dancing show horse or one that jumped those impossibly high obstacles, just for a silver cup or a ribbon. I wanted a horse that would take me across open fields at a fast gallop, simply because he loved to run.

The black stallion

In my mind I had wandered far from Mrs Kemp's table, but she brought me back abruptly when she said, 'Well now, let's talk about Splash.'

Suddenly, I felt afraid again as I was reminded why I was there.

'I am very sorry I took your horse, Mrs Kemp, I will never do it again,' I said with downcast eyes.

'No, I don't think you will,' she murmured thoughtfully. 'I believe your father thrashed you pretty badly last night?'

I didn't answer, I just stared at my hands folded in my lap.

'Well, I guess you have been punished enough,' she said briskly. 'Now let's get down to business. How would you like to come and work for me?'

I stared at her.

'You want to give me a job?' I asked, incredulous.

Mrs Kemp nodded her head.

She leaned back in her chair and, with a faraway look in her eyes, said, 'We haven't had any good rain for quite some time now. Heaven knows there's precious little feed in the paddocks, so I need someone to take the horses out every day and graze them in the open, then bring them home again in the afternoon. Do you think you could do that?'

I nodded my head vigorously, not trusting myself to speak. I thought I might cry with happiness.

Mrs Kemp leaned forward across the table and stared into my face.

'It is a very responsible job being in charge of a mob of horses, do you think you can do it?'

'Yes,' I replied, 'I can, and I know I will enjoy this job very much.'

'Good,' she said. 'You can start the day after tomorrow. In the meantime, you can take Splash home. See that you both rest up a bit. Go on, off you go.' She shooed me out the door. 'I've got work to do.'

As I left Mrs Kemp's house, I tried to walk normally, tried not to let her see how sore I was.

Many Lifetimes

∞

Those were some of the happiest days of my life. I felt very special being in charge of so many horses. I grazed the mob over crown land, along the roadside and down into dry creek-beds where some of the horses liked to roll in the sand. There were magic moments too, when I would find a cool shady place beside a small creek where the horses could drink and nibble at the tender green shoots of grass.

But then, somehow, a different day came.

That afternoon was warm and hazy and, as I lay down in the cool grass, I began to daydream. I fantasised that Splash was a beautiful, bold black stallion, who would let me ride upon his back without saddle or bridle and together we would lead a band of wild horses across the never-ending plains.

In my mind's eye, I saw the black stallion standing on a high rocky outcrop on the edge of the plains. He was a magnificent creature and lord and master of a band of wild mares and foals grazing peacefully below. I didn't own the stallion, nobody did, nobody ever could, he was a free spirit, a creature of nature, and to attempt to tame him would destroy the very qualities I admired.

As he stood there outlined against the blue sky, he turned his proud, regal head towards me. I saw the muscles of his powerful chest and shoulders ripple beneath his black, glossy coat. Then, with a defiant toss of his head and a flick of his black, flying tail, he was gone, to reappear almost immediately around the spur of the hill. I felt a quiver of fear as a ton of black thunder galloped towards me. Still, I held my ground and when he was only a few yards away he propped, his forelegs stiffly out in front, forcing his hindquarters back upon their haunches. Slowly, tossing his head from side to side in greeting, he walked towards me. There was a soft guttural sound coming from deep within his chest. I looked into his brown eyes, and saw a kindred spirit, a fellow rebel.

With the ease of a gazelle, I leapt upon his back and we became one, the stallion and me, running wild and free like the wind. I saw the band of wild mares and foals join us as we flew past them, our stride long and sure-footed. I thrilled to the sound of our hooves thudding on the ground, echoing like drums into the distance behind us. Then I fell asleep.

It was almost dark when I awoke, and there was no sign of the horses.

Only Splash remained and I was glad I had tethered him with a rope. Frantically, panic-stricken, I rode back to the stables hoping that the horses had returned home by themselves. They weren't there, but Mrs Kemp was.

'You're late!' she shouted angrily. 'Where are the horses?'

It took two days to round them up. They had split into several groups, creating a hazard to traffic. A couple were picked up by the council pound. I lost my job.

I never saw Splash again.

Part Two

February 1948

Panic attacks, aged 14

I was in a boat. It was rising and falling and being tossed around by a huge and angry sea. I tried to grip the sides to stop myself from being thrown into the water but I couldn't move my hands. Something was holding me by my wrists. Was it my father? I could hear his voice but I couldn't see him through the dense grey fog. Suddenly I realised there was something wrong with my eyes – I couldn't open them. Was this some awful dream? I could feel the sickness and panic rising within me as I struggled to see. Now my eyes opened to slits and I saw my father a long way off on an island, talking to some people in white coats. He was wearing his blue suit.

My father just had one suit and he only wore it on special or official occasions. I knew he was here on very serious business. More clearly now I could hear him shouting and pointing to me, his face was thunderous. I began to cry. I thought he was angry with me and I was in big trouble. He looked at me then, and – in an instant, I don't know how he did it – somehow he had leaped across the raging sea and was there beside me.

'Don't cry, Freddie,' he said softly as he untied my hands from the rails around the bed. 'They've been giving you drugs and I am taking you out of here.'

He wrapped a blanket around me, scooped me up in his arms, and carried me across the room. When we got to the door, it was locked.

'Open this bloody door right now before I kick it down,' my father said in a cold, deliberate voice.

I had never seen him like this, and I was glad he was not angry with me. Slowly the door opened. A doctor stood there barring the way.

'Mr May, your daughter is very ill, she is urgently in need of treatment,' he said.

'Get out of the way,' my father replied menacingly. 'I'm taking her home.'

'You're making a big mistake, Mr May. Audrey is suffering from severe depression and is potentially suicidal.'

'Move,' my father hissed through clenched teeth.

'Well, if you insist, but you will need to sign a release form before you go, absolving the hospital of any further responsibility.'

That was too much for my father; he pushed past the doctor and we left the hospital without further incident.

∞

At first, my father treated me at home with brandy, just a teaspoon every two hours. Then Sedna Wine, a mild sedative, which the chemist assured him would cure nervous depression. It did not. My condition did not improve, so a local doctor was called in. This doctor prescribed paraldehyde to alleviate depression.

I was heavily sedated most of the time and this drug positively ruled out any possibility of my being able to work. It kept me in a dreamlike state, where I had no uncontrollable rages or crying fits of depression. However, the downside was that the paraldehyde made my whole body stink, even if I could not smell it myself. The odour exuded offensively from the pores of my skin. My sisters unkindly complained that I was a walking sewer. At these times I was ashamed and embarrassed. My father, who was notorious for his blunt, often cruel manner of speaking, would say, 'Phew, you're ripe, Fred, go and hose yourself down.'

I can never remember my mother ever being unkind to me, though. She would say things like, 'Go and have a rest, Freddie, and when you get up, I will run a nice hot bath for you.' I loved her for her kindness and gentle understanding.

June 1948

Ward Sixteen

> *Big nose Jan went to bed,*
> *With a cold in her head,*
> *She used the sheet to blow her nose,*
> *Now the sheet is full of holes.*
>
> (A. May)

I was returned to Ward Sixteen, the psychiatric ward of the Brisbane General Hospital, several more times after this. During my last stay there, I wrote a great deal. Sometimes I wrote short stories and composed poems. At other times, I wrote silly idiotic rhymes about the hospital staff. Nurses, doctors, patients and at times the servery and cleaning staff, all fell victim to my pen. I liked to study people secretly. Then, using their physical deficiencies or mannerisms, I would amuse myself by penning a few lines about their pointy noses or big bums. Not all of my rhymes were benign; some were downright offensive. These I destroyed by flushing them down the toilet before anyone could read them. However, I did begin to write poetry that was more serious.

I had quickly learned through experience that staffers had power over patients and it didn't pay to offend them. So, after a few narrow escapes – nurses wanting to read what I had written – I decided to write something I could show them to satisfy their curiosity.

I had read an article in a magazine about the practice of the South American Indians of tipping their blow darts, arrows and spears with the poison 'curare'. This poisonous plant grew naturally in the jungle and was readily available to the natives. Curare would effectively paralyse the motor nerves of an animal or person, immobilising them. Death would quickly follow, due to asphyxiation.

I decided to write a murder mystery, using curare as a murder weapon.

My story was set in Australia, and the plot was built around the death of an old lady who grew prize roses. She was found dead in her garden; the coroner's verdict, death from asphyxiation. A neighbour, who also happened to be an amateur sleuth, uncovered the existence of the little-known poison curare that had been applied to the thorns of the roses. He solved the crime and brought the murderer to justice.

The psychiatrist in charge of my case in Ward Sixteen read my story with interest and later told my father that I was highly intelligent. This was the last time I was in the Brisbane General Hospital. Thereafter I was sent directly to the Goodna Mental Hospital.

The accident

When we were young it was common for the neighbourhood kids to frequent the local dump, and although the smell must have been terrible we didn't seem to mind. To the poor the dump was a treasure trove of forbidden delights, particularly as the American army dumped truckloads of unopened cartons of sweets such as Hoadley Violet Crumble bars and the like. There were cartons of Wrigley's chewing gum, and an endless range of lollies. I never understood why they were so wasteful, but everyone knew the Yanks had pots of money and could afford the very best. Mum said maybe the lollies were old, but they still tasted good to me. Nevertheless, we were careful not to eat anything that was not properly sealed.

One day while playing hide and seek at the dump, my brother Patrick and I found a rusty old ship's container and decided to hide inside it. It was about six feet square and just as deep. Patrick let himself down into the tank without any trouble. However, I hung on to the edge of the container, with my head still visible above it, refusing to let go.

'Hurry up and let go, they can still see you,' Patrick said.

But I was almost in tears. 'I can't, I'm too scared.'

What Patrick did next was something he was to regret for the rest of his life. A normally harmless act, it would have far-reaching consequences for us both. He tickled me under the arms.

I let go of the side of the container and, as I dropped inside, my two front teeth caught on the edge of the container and broke off.

Over the next few months, my upper teeth began to loosen and, one by one, they fell out. My father said I would be without teeth for the rest of my life. He said I would never be able to wear dentures as my mouth was deformed. Patrick didn't hear this, though, as he had gone bush.

No specialist opinion was ever sought. My father just said, 'You only have to look at her bucked teeth to see how deformed her mouth is.'

To be told at fifteen years old that I would have to face the world with a gummy mouth for the rest of my life was more than I could bear.

January 1950

The milk factory

For a year after I had my teeth broken off, I just stayed at home and helped Mum. When there was just Mum and me at home we would talk and laugh together.

But by the time I was nearly sixteen, I seemed a lot better.

As soon as Dad saw I was well again, he told me to go out and find a job, to support myself.

∞

I was too embarrassed to work in milkbars or restaurants, or anywhere I had to face the public, but Dad insisted. So I applied for a job at Pauls' milk factory. I was able to get the 3 a.m. shift, during which, apart from the girls I worked with, I had very little contact with anyone.

The work there was hard, uninteresting, or downright boring.

After a while I was assigned to the loading dock to replace the regular girl, who was on sick leave.

When I met Ian Lane I was sixteen. He owned his own milk delivery run, and I was flattered when he paid me a lot of attention even though I didn't have any upper teeth. Ian was eight years my senior, good-looking and charming, and I felt complimented, too, by the attention of an older man. But I resisted him for some time.

I had a great fear of men. It took a lot of courage for me to agree to go out with him. Even then we didn't go anywhere. We just drove to a deserted spot. Ian said, 'I want to be alone with you. I don't want to share you with anyone else.' And I believed him.

We consumed a great deal of alcohol on those nights. Sometimes I didn't even remember getting home. But our romance was short-lived. After only a few weeks I was transferred to the bottling machine. I would see Ian Lane only once again.

∞

When my brother Patrick came home from the bush after about a year there, he was shocked to see that I still didn't have any upper teeth.

'Why hasn't Audrey got any false teeth?' he asked my father.

'Because her mouth is deformed and she can't wear them,' Dad replied.

'How do you know?' Patrick asked. 'Has she been to a dentist?'

'No, but you saw what her teeth were like, she couldn't possibly wear dentures.'

'We'll see about that,' said Patrick.

I knew Patrick was feeling guilty because he had caused the accident, though I had never blamed him. It was, after all, an accident and not as if he *meant* to hurt me. But he was very angry with my father for not doing anything about it.

The next day Patrick took me to a dentist who had rooms in a building on the corner of Queen and George streets in the city. The dentist examined me and, to our delight, he pronounced the formation of my mouth perfectly normal. He set about taking impressions for a new set of dentures and soon I was wearing new teeth with pride.

Patrick paid for them out of his own money – I think they cost sixteen pounds.

I did not know

I would probably never have known I was pregnant, until the birth, except for an incident at Pauls' milk factory, where I was still working the early shift.

During a short early morning break, I accidentally came upon a group of women in the bottle-washing department. They were huddled around a young girl who was crying. Curious, I stopped to listen. I overheard the girl say, 'I only went to the doctor because my periods had stopped, and he told me I was going to have a baby.'

Periods stopped... having a baby... these words echoed and re-echoed through my brain. The realisation of why I no longer got periods dawned upon me.

Slowly at first, like the cold grey light of day, followed by the warm flush of morning, gaining momentum, the heat spread throughout my body, burning into my brain, my heart and lungs, until it reached the surface of my skin, where it cooled, leaving me cold and clammy and shivering more with fear than cold.

A spasm gripped my throat as I tried to hold back the tears. I didn't want the women to question me, so I quickly retrieved my handbag from the locker in the lunchroom and, muttering something to the supervisor about being unwell, I left the building. I walked unsteadily to the nearby bank of the Brisbane River, at the rear of the factory. There in the grey early light, I sat and stared into the water. I tried desperately to still the racing of my heart and the roaring in my ears. How, I asked myself, if I *was* pregnant, could it have happened? I wasn't a bad girl and people said girls who got pregnant before they were married were bad women who slept around with anyone. I didn't do that.

So maybe I wasn't pregnant. But I knew I was clutching at straws – the swelling of my body and the stopping of my periods spoke for themselves.

I was going to have a baby. When or how this was to happen had not yet occurred to me.

By the time the first rays of the sun appeared in the sky, I still had no idea what I should do, which wasn't surprising, as I didn't even know what my options were.

Slowly, laboriously, I got to my feet. I didn't know it then, but I was already six months pregnant. My father had often remarked, over the previous few months, how much weight I was putting on, but this was attributed to my indulgence in the rich dairy products at the factory.

I certainly did not look pregnant. I had what Mum called a roly-poly figure, and carried my weight evenly distributed around my body, so this was deceiving.

Reluctantly, I made my way home.

Still Sixteen

The fifties were draconian times

At this time I did not think of the child within me as my own baby or a real child. I had no maternal instinct to love and protect it. I felt as if a foreign object had invaded my body. Perhaps it was the sneakiness of having something growing inside of you without your knowledge or consent that made me afraid.

I didn't even know what I had to do to have a baby. I wished somebody had told me what was going to happen to me. I was terrified. You see, I had no idea how I was going to get it out of my body. The only way I could think of was through the navel. It seemed to serve no other purpose.

At no time did it occur to me that a baby might emerge from my 'pee-hole'. It isn't surprising that I was ignorant of the process of childbirth, when I wasn't even sure how a baby had got there in the first place.

I was not the only one who was pitifully naive, sexually uneducated and uninformed. Ignorance among young people on all matters to do with sex and the reproductive organs was typical of the 1950s. Young girls married, completely unaware of what was expected of them on their wedding night. Some young virginal boys and girls coming together were psychologically and physically unprepared to deal with their sexuality. They found their inhibitions, born of a lifetime of taboos, too difficult to overcome.

The forbidden heavy petting on the back seat of the FJ Holden (parked in Lovers' Lane) was fun. The kissing, the groping and heavy breathing (although we were told kissing alone could lead to pregnancy) were a whole world away from what was to come – the bedroom scene. Newly married women, particularly teenagers, seeing an erect male sex organ coming across the room towards them, lost all the romantic notions of the blushing bride and, thoroughly traumatised, went tearfully home to Mother.

The 1950s was an era of secrets, distrust, hypocrisy and false modesty; an era of lies and deceit, when stern matrons gave warnings of doom without explanations, for fear that if young women were told how to avoid sexual pitfalls it might lead them to be more secretly immoral. Girls from wealthy families, who also often found themselves pregnant, suddenly took extended holidays to visit a little-known aunt, and returned no longer pregnant and without the child. Some families pursued dangerous practices such as secret home births in order to maintain the family's squeaky-clean reputation. These were indeed draconian times and they claimed many victims.

I had never visited a doctor, let alone been examined. I

was afraid of the doctor's scorn and I could imagine him saying, 'You're having an illegitimate child? Shame on you, you worthless hussy, I don't treat persons of such low morals.' So I was too ashamed to let anyone know I was pregnant. I just went on pretending there was nothing wrong.

It was like an electricity bill that you can't afford to pay, and you put it in a drawer hoping the problem will go away, until one night you find yourself sitting in the dark.

That dark time came when I was eight months pregnant.

My sister Helen

As I sat alone deep in thought in my bedroom, the dim moonlight coming through the window, I saw my door open; just a little at first, then a head appeared, followed after a moment by the rest of a body. It was my older sister Helen.

'Can we talk?' she whispered.

I was taken by surprise; Helen never bothered with me unless she had to. Nevertheless, at that moment I was pleased to have someone to talk to.

I watched as she sat carefully on the end of the bed, the pale light playing in her hair, turning a single strand here and there from black to silver and back again.

For a long moment we just sat there, saying nothing. Helen gazed past me and seemed preoccupied with the lemon tree outside the window. As I waited, I studied her face, like I was seeing it for the first time. She had a flawless olive complexion and dark arched eyebrows, framed by a tousled mass of soft, curly black hair. She was an attractive young girl, and already married with a baby of her own.

Watching, I noticed her full lips were parted and moving slightly, as if she were rehearsing a role she was about to play. Then, as if on cue, she turned her face towards me and said, 'Freddie, are you in trouble?'

I hadn't realised I was holding my breath, until it came out in a deep sigh.

'Yes,' I replied. 'I am in trouble, big trouble.'

Helen started interrogating me then. 'When is the baby due?'

'I don't know.'

'How many months pregnant are you?'

'I don't know.'

'Have you seen a doctor?'

'No.'

'Why not?'

'Because I was frightened and ashamed,' I told her truthfully.

'Who is the father?'

This I did know. 'The milkman,' I replied confidently, and not without irony.

'Stop trying to be funny, Freddie, don't you realise how serious this is?' Helen snapped. I could see she was close to tears.

'I'm not being funny,' I answered defensively. 'Ian Lane is the milkman I met at the factory, where I work.'

'How do you know it was him that made you pregnant?'

I turned away and looked out the window, my bravado ebbing away.

This was the strange part. I didn't know how I had got pregnant, but my meagre knowledge of sex and reproduction informed me that it took a man to make a woman pregnant, even if only through kissing.

'Because,' I replied wearily, 'Ian Lane is the only man I have ever gone out with.'

I was only half-aware that my sister had left the room.

Crown Street Women's Hospital

I awoke with the sun high in the sky, my heart heavy as I prepared to face yet another bad day. Now I thought of an article I had previously read – an article in the *Women's Weekly* about Matron Shaw of the Crown Street Women's Hospital in Sydney, who took in young unmarried mothers and cared for them until their babies were born. My sister and I decided that this was the only option I had. I couldn't tell my parents, such would be the shame visited upon them. I would rather leave home than face the disappointment of my mother, and the terrible anger of my father.

Helen and I packed a bag for me, then went to see Ian Lane, who admitted paternity but refused to marry me. He did, however, offer to pay my plane fare to Sydney.

We booked a one-way ticket to Sydney the same day. After I had said goodbye to Helen, she went home to break the news to my parents.

Peter

When the taxi stopped at the front entrance of the Crown Street Women's Hospital in Sydney, I was alone and afraid. As I stood there on the footpath with the total sum of threepence in my pocket, and everything I owned shoved into an old cardboard suitcase, I was very afraid and close to tears.

I entered the hospital and asked at the desk for Matron Shaw. But the unthinkable happened: I was told she was away on leave and wouldn't be back for several weeks.

I was stunned. It had never occurred to me that Matron Shaw would not be there. The article had led me to believe that if I could only get to the hospital I would get help. I didn't have a plan B.

'Oh, okay,' I said, in as matter-of-fact a way as I could muster. 'I'll come back later.' I picked up my port and left the hospital.

I was back on the footpath when I felt someone touch my shoulder. A young nurse in a blue and white uniform was standing there. I knew she was speaking to me – I saw her lips moving – but I couldn't hear her voice, there was a terrible roaring in my ears. Then the noise in my head stopped.

'. . . would you like to do that?' I heard her saying.

'Do what?' I asked stupidly.

'Come back inside,' she said. 'Sister Kerns wants to talk to you.' As if that settled the matter, she picked up my port and started walking back inside the hospital gates.

∞

Once admitted to the hospital I was regarded more as a fallen woman than a young girl in need of friendship and understanding. From the day I arrived, I was treated with derision, and pressured by nursing staff, doctors and various visiting welfare and religious groups to give my baby up for adoption. They made it quite clear that the only interest they had in me was the baby I was carrying.

I went into labour on 4 September at 5 a.m. Even at the hospital nobody had talked to me about what it was like to have a baby or prepared me for the birth. I still didn't know what was going to happen to me. After a gruelling twenty-four hours of labour I felt my stomach drop down – and all I could think of was that my entire insides were about to drop out. I tightened all my muscles, unaware that I might be killing the baby.

Eventually, though, my child came safely into the world and was taken away before I could see him.

I watched as other mothers delightedly received their babies. The joy of motherhood was filling their faces with sunshine.

Despite the long and difficult birth, I looked forward eagerly to seeing my child for the first time. But as time passed, with the sound of the stiffly starched blue and white uniforms of the nurses passing by my bed, to and fro with babies – none of them mine – I began to think that maybe my baby had died. Suddenly, the child I had not wanted before the birth became the most important person in the world to me.

Seeing me upset, a nurse came over. 'Is my baby dead?' I asked tearfully.

'No, of course not,' she replied reassuringly, 'but Matron wants to talk to you before you see him, that's all. She will be here in just a few moments. Better not let her see you so upset,' she added conspiratorially.

I was not allowed to see my baby until much later.

When I refused to sign the adoption papers that were shoved in front of me I was accused of selfishness. Of depriving my child of the respectability of belonging to rich, well-adjusted, God-fearing parents. How could I contemplate being a single mother with an illegitimate child, did I have no shame?

Adoptive parents were seen then as squeaky clean, respectable – worthier than I was. I was told that in a few months I would have forgotten about my baby and would be able to marry and have more children. And, 'What kind of man would want to marry a girl with another man's baby?' But I wouldn't budge.

I didn't tell them that I didn't want to marry, that I saw the institution of marriage as just that, an institution. I had seen what happened when you entered the hallowed halls of matrimony. You gave up all rights to your own person. You became the 'other half' – as opposed to the 'better half', or 'the little woman' – and obedient slave of the 'head of the house'. Failure to conform to the high ideals of matrimony in the 1950s meant violent physical battering. Why would I want to marry? Now seventeen, I thought I knew it all.

∞

When my mother arrived at the hospital to take me home, the pressure accelerated, as she too was intimidated. The onus was now on my mum to make me see reason. Her own suitability as a mother was called into question. 'What sort of mother would have a daughter with an illegitimate baby in her home? Did she have no shame?'

Then came the sweeteners.

The offers to train me as a nurse – and my mother saw this perhaps as some form of salvation for me – but I would have to give up my baby. Mum tried to persuade me to have him adopted and become a nurse, but I wouldn't budge. Finally Mum gave in.

This was the experience for young defenceless girls at the mercy of unscrupulous baby marketeers.

Babies

When Mum and I arrived home from Sydney with my little son, he was just five days old. He instantly became the star attraction in our household. My father adored him and dubbed him Peter after his grandfather.

All day, my parents and my sisters would nurse and play with him and Helen's baby. Peter was never put straight to bed to take his nap (he didn't have a cot, there was no room for one), but was always soothed according to Mum's instructions: cradled in the arms and held snugly against the breast. 'Babies must always feel physically safe and secure, or they will sleep fretfully and wake ill-tempered,' Mum repeatedly reminded us. The girls and I would complain, 'We know, Mum, you've told us over and over again.'

'Yes,' she would say, 'and I'll tell you again and again and again – until you learn. Then you can never say,' (Mum placed her hands one on each side of her head, mouth wide open, her eyes rolled back, posturing in mock horror,) '"Oh! I forgot!"'

Mum was right, of course. 'Forgetting' was a catchcry of ours and we used it relentlessly to excuse our carelessness.

But Peter never wanted for anything.

∞

I breast-fed Peter until he was six months old. I remember one day when I was in the city looking for work, I missed the bus home. I was frantic because it was already past the hour when Peter was due to be fed.

I caught the next bus and all the way home I was worried about him crying with hunger, and Mum would be angry too. 'Have you forgotten you have a little baby that relies on you to feed him?' she would say. 'Don't you realise you're a woman now, not a child, and you should be more responsible?'

Suddenly I was no longer seventeen. I had a baby and that made me an instant adult.

Spurred on by these thoughts I jumped off the bus at my stop and sprinted the short distance home. When I burst through the front door, out of breath, all hot and sweaty, and dreading the dressing-down I knew was coming, my mother and my sister Helen were sitting at the kitchen table talking quietly. Peter was asleep on Mum's lap.

I was dumbfounded.

Mum got to her feet and handed the sleeping baby to Helen, saying, 'Look at the state you're in! Your milk will be boiling. Come and sit down here,' indicating the chair she had just vacated. She then bustled around, getting me first a glass of water, which I drank immediately, then a bowl of cool water and a face cloth. Mum sponged my face, neck and wrists. Nobody seemed to have noticed that I hadn't spoken, but I truly didn't know what to say. Then Mum said, 'And don't you worry about Peter, he's been fed and now he's sleeping contentedly.'

All I could say was, 'What did he have?' I couldn't believe Mum would give him cows' milk.

'Oh, it's all right, Helen fed him.' And they both burst out laughing.

Then it became clear: Helen, with her own baby, had an over-abundance of breast milk. Mum and Helen thought it was a huge joke.

∞

So Peter had a plentiful supply of mothers; he barely had time to wet his pants before Mum or my sisters would be running for a clean nappy. The bathing, changing and dressing was usually a combined effort. Mum, the only one with experience, would supervise my younger sisters' efforts at playing the little mother. One would fetch the nappy (these were already folded ready for use as soon as they came in from the clothesline). Another would have a warm moist cloth, while yet another administered the Johnson's Baby Powder. Mum, of course, had charge of the nappy pins. No one but Mum, Helen and myself was allowed to 'pin the nappy up', for fear of sticking the babies with a pin. I first had to undergo rigorous training before I was allowed to pin-up unaided. Mum was forever saying to me and Helen,

'Always put your hand inside the nappy, so if the pin goes in too far it will jab your hand and not the baby.' The girls didn't like the thought of being jabbed with a vicious weapon like a pin and were happy to leave the pinning-up to someone else.

It isn't hard to see why Peter was a happy, contented baby. That is, during the day. It was a different story at night, though. Perhaps Peter was so used to being lulled to sleep in somebody's arms, listening to the soft crooning voice, and that special sound he had heard even before he was born, the rhythm of a beating heart, that when he woke at night, he missed all the attention, and became fretful.

That's when Dad would play his part. He too loved to spoil Peter. He jokingly called him 'Barnes Auto' (a towing company who are still in business today). Their motto is *We Never Sleep.* Almost every night when Peter cried, Dad would come and pick him up, saying to me, 'Go back to sleep, Freddie, I'll take care of him.'

Dad never complained when he walked the floor with Peter at night. First it was wind, then teething or fever. It was a special time Dad shared with his grandchild. I would hear him talking to Peter, in a voice and tone I had never heard him use before. It was a sort of soft, conspiratorial, one-sided conversation that one might have with an adult. I could never actually hear what Dad was saying and, in a way, I didn't want to. I was just grateful that my parents welcomed us back into the home that I had left in disgrace.

Part Three

Eighteen Years Old

The house

One day I overheard my father and mother talking about household finances. I knew Peter and I were an added burden to them and I wished I could help, but what with Peter, and my history and not being able to hold a regular job, I seemed unemployable. Dad was on unemployment benefits and they were having a hard time making ends meet. Nevertheless, we were well fed and clothed – nothing fancy but certainly adequate.

Still, I decided to earn some money the best way I could.

∞

The house at number 1 Drake Street was located at the far end of a small, dead-end street in West End. It was in an industrial area and, during the day, workmen saw the clients arrive in taxis. At the top of a long staircase, enclosed on three sides with corrugated iron, a small chain-wire gate barred the entrance. The men would begin lining up on the stairs from about six o'clock in the evening.

There were always at least one or two of the young, hairless variety of the male species sitting on the footpath with their backs to the corrugated-iron fence. When I asked what they were doing there, I was told by Peg Connor, the madam, that they were either first-timers trying to pluck up the courage to come in or, perhaps more frequently, they were just too young and knew they wouldn't be allowed in.

In the evening it was Peg Connor who opened the wire gate, around seven o'clock. She was identifiable as the madam because she didn't wear the same evening gown as the workers. Peg Connor wore a smart after-five cocktail dress and a false, brittle smile that died before reaching her eyes. She greeted the men as they came through the door: 'Good evening, gentlemen, just go through the first door on your right.'

The white dress

When I went to the house to get a job, I was told I needed a long evening gown to wear. So I went shopping in McDonnell and East for the material. The fabric I chose was a shiny taffeta with pink and green flowers sprinkled over a background of white. I thought it was very pretty. To avoid having to explain why the dress had to be made in a certain way, we all went to the same dressmaker.

When I took my fabric to the dressmaker, she said, 'Oh, but it's so pretty and girlish.' I was puzzled. Her words said one thing, yet her tone said something else.

'Thank you,' I said, a little uncertainly, 'I think it's nice too.'

Then she said, 'You will need a plunging neckline to reveal as much cleavage as possible.' Looking down at myself, I thought my under-developed breasts and cleavage would hardly excite anyone. 'Then a long open-ended zipper to fasten the bodice, to about four or five inches below the waist. From there the skirt will billow out and be completely open to the hem.'

'Could I have puffed sleeves?' I asked timidly.

'No, no!' It was a stern reply. 'Men like to see your armpits,' she added, looking at me oddly.

My demure youthful gown amused the madam and my co-workers. I was told it was a party dress rather than a sex worker's gown. It was in total contrast to the deep reds, blacks and dark blue satins and laces of the other girls. Certainly no pastel shades were ever seen. I soon learned, however, that these colours were specifically worn to make a statement. I didn't find out until later that men who came to these houses were looking for the experienced woman who could give them value for money.

My working name was Jessie, and with my party dress and youthful appearance, fear and uncertainty showing on my face – well, in spite of what anyone may think, I was not in high demand.

The girls, as they were ironically called (their ages ranged from late twenties up to forty), sat on dining-room chairs in the large sitting room and waited for the madam to appear in the doorway with her fixed smile and ask, 'Ready, girls?' This was the signal for the girls to extinguish their cigarettes, cease talking, sit up straight, and swirl their long skirts around to form a frame for their bare, crossed legs.

The girls' faces would be transformed into the image they wanted to convey to the client who would desire their special sexual talents. Not all girls would take all clients. Those who wanted deviant sex, such as oral or anal sex or bondage, would ask for or choose girls who offered these services. Each girl was at liberty to refuse a client because of what she considered abnormal sexual practices. After all, some of them had husbands and boyfriends to go home to.

Some girls cultivated their natural colouring and good looks to create a specific image. The man who wanted to be enslaved by a woman would choose the dark-haired, sloe-eyed, high-priestess type, who would tie him up and whip him into submission. However, these were special cases. Mostly, the men just wanted sex.

The prices ranged from two pounds for seven minutes, known as 'a short time', to five pounds for half an hour. Some men stayed for an hour and paid ten pounds. Less frequently, there were the overnighters who stayed for a cost of twenty pounds. (This type of client was not encouraged; for security reasons, at least one other girl had to stay in the house if a client wanted to spend the night with a girl.)

Men loved these surreal encounters. While their body enjoyed sexual gratification, in their minds their fantasies were brought to life and the girls became whoever and whatever they wanted. There was always someone who could accommodate their wildest dreams, provided they had the money to pay for it. But I had no such image and I wasn't interested enough to develop one.

∞

One day the madam asked if I would take a special client whose requirement was bondage. I'd had a few drinks and although I agreed (he was a regular of a girl who was not available at this time), I was very much afraid of him. His manner indicated that he was an inoffensive person; his eyes revealed nothing. That in itself disturbed me. It was as if a veil had been drawn across the window of his soul, making him unreadable. I got the distinct feeling that I was being watched but could not see the watcher. I shrugged it off. If I freaked out every time I met a cuckoo then I would never make any money.

Nevertheless, when he opened the little black case he carried and started to extract objects of torture – a short riding crop, a thin wooden cane, leather straps, a small piece of smooth wood about four inches long, tapered at both ends (I worried about that) and finally a long pair of black leather boots with high heels – I could scarcely contain my revulsion and fear. I was scared, and there was no way I was going to let him tie me up.

I watched as he stripped off his clothes, carefully folding them and laying them down upon the only chair in the room. Then, ever so slowly, his smooth white plump little body moved across to the bed. As he lay down on his back staring up at the ceiling, I noticed his body was glistening with moisture. Silently he waited.

All this time I had been standing with my back to the door, my hand tightly clutching the door handle, ready to get out fast if things turned nasty. Adrenalin coursing through my body and my throat dry and constricted, I was mesmerised by that wet white lump of human flesh on the bed, laid out like a corpse. Then I became aware that there was something wrong with this corpse. Suddenly it came to me. He had no penis.

I panicked. Fled. Got out of that place as fast as I could.

∞

I went to the pub and got drunk – or rather, drunker.

I was arrested for being drunk in a public place. I was sent right back to the mental hospital.

Goodna Mental Hospital

The way shock treatment was given in those days was nothing less than cruel and barbaric. Even back on the paraldehyde, I was so traumatised by simply seeing the treatment, I wished I could die before they got to me. In the large dormitory, each patient was lined up in their little beds, lying on top of the sad grey blankets as, one by one, they received the dreaded treatment.

I watched as six nurses held down each patient on the

bed, while another swabbed their temples with a saline solution. The mouth was forced open and a piece of rubber hose was placed between the teeth. Finally, the steel plates – which would send the electric current burning and stabbing into their brain – were placed on the temples.

The current was switched on.

As I listened to the screams of each patient as they convulsed for several seconds, I became more terrified, until finally I jumped up from my bed and ran from the ward.

After this I was locked in a cell and given shock treatment alone on my bed.

∞

I never ever recovered from the memory of having shock treatment. I suffered nightmares for years. They always started the same: my bedroom door would be thrown open and many people in blue hospital uniforms would rush, in slow motion, towards my bed.

Mostly I woke myself up screaming or sometimes falling out of the bed.

Peg Connor

After about two weeks, I was told I was being released into my mother's care. However, when I was taken to the reception room I saw only the madam, Peg Connor, standing there smiling at me. At first, I thought she had posed as my mother to get me out of the hospital. Then I saw my mother get up from the seat beside her. I could not believe my mother and Peg Connor were in the same room, let alone together.

Peg Connor's presence seemed to fill the room, so I was unable to see anyone else. I shrank back as she came towards me.

'My dear,' she said – smiling sweetly while her eyes drilled holes in me.

Peg Connor wanted me to return to the house with her, but I refused. I just wanted to go home with my mother.

I still could not believe my mother was there with the madam.

1953

The abortion

I had been at home only a few weeks when I found out I was pregnant again. I was nineteen, and the abortion would be one of the most frightening and soul-destroying episodes of my life... not only the abortion, but also the two-year delay from the abortion to the actual burial of the aborted child.

My son Peter was still very young. My parents had borne the shame of having their unmarried daughter with an illegitimate child in their home and I knew the stigma of another would be a cruel blow to them. I couldn't hurt them again like that. Besides, I knew I was not well enough to care for another child. I had no job, no money, and my nerves were very bad. I knew it would be better if I didn't have the child, so I took the only course I felt was open to me.

I learned the method from a girl who had successfully performed an abortion on herself. That night, in the small hours of the morning, I quietly crept out of bed, went to the laundry and got a bucket. I collected the cake of Castile soap and my mother's douche can from the bathroom and carried it all out to the kitchen. It's not clear to me why I wanted to do this terrible thing in the kitchen instead of the bathroom. Perhaps I just wasn't thinking rationally, or perhaps deep down I was hoping that I would be discovered. God knows I didn't want to do it. I had been warned that it was dangerous, but I don't think I cared if I died. Maybe I thought I deserved to die anyway.

So there, within a few feet of my parents' bedroom door, I penetrated to the womb with the nozzle of the syringe. I felt a sharp pain shoot through my body. I fell backwards, tipping the bucket over. Water spread all over the floor. In a haze of pain and fear, I tried to mop up with towels . . . then I went to bed.

Some time later I awoke, excruciating pain tearing through my stomach. I felt nauseated and thought I was going to die.

Carefully, I got out of bed.

I was freezing cold and overwhelmed with sickness and dizziness. I wanted to go to the toilet, but it was outside, way up the backyard, so I made my way to the bathroom. I didn't get to the wash basin, however, before I was sick all over my pyjamas and myself.

Our shower was over the bathtub, so I took off my clothes and stepped into the bath and turned on the shower. The pain was getting worse and I felt like screaming. Suddenly, I felt all my insides drop out. I looked down and saw blood gushing out of me, rushing towards the plughole and forming a red whirlpool.

I knew I had to do something, but I didn't know what. I was mesmerised by all the blood and placenta. I stood there staring at it, thinking maybe I was dreaming and, if I stood there long enough, I would wake up and everything would be all right.

But it didn't go away and finally I tried to push the mess down the drain. It wouldn't go through, and that is when I found it.

Small and white, about four inches long, a perfectly formed, translucent baby boy.

I picked him up and gently cradled him in my hands before I laid the tiny form of my child on a white towel. As I gazed down upon him, I thought how like an angel he looked nestled on a snowy white cloud.

∞

With tears streaming down my face, for the second time that night I fetched the bucket from the laundry and filled it with the solid matter from the bathtub. It was an unpleasant and gruesome task.

I now had to take the bucket up to the backyard to the outdoor toilet, empty the contents into the pan and cover it well with sawdust.

But I couldn't under any circumstances put my tiny baby into the toilet.

As I returned to the house and went to pass my parents' room, I saw a crack of light under the door, which meant that at least one of my parents was awake. I was paralysed with fear, afraid I would be discovered. Suddenly, I realised I was still naked and spattered with blood.

Then the light went out and I noiselessly returned to the bathroom. I knew I had to decide what I would do with the baby. First I would name him and then I would give him a decent burial.

∞

I called my unborn child *Ben*. Ben, because it is such a strong and powerful, yet gentle name, and that is exactly what I imagined he would have been, if he had been allowed to live. I wanted to bury Ben in the garden, under the passionfruit vine near the fence. He wasn't likely to be disturbed there. But I saw that it was breaking day, and people would be moving about, so I decided to postpone the burial until later that night. In the meantime, I would preserve his little body. I slipped out to the kitchen and got a clean, empty jar, filled it with methylated spirits, slipped the little limp body inside and screwed on the metal lid.

The bottle with its precious contents could not be discovered before I had a chance to bury it, so I had to find a place to hide it.

In my room, a built-in wardrobe reached up to the ceiling. At the top, there was a cupboard the furthermost recesses of which could only be reached by climbing inside. There I hid the bottle, fully intending to retrieve it that night.

For the next few days, however, I was very ill and too weak to get out of bed. I managed to convince my parents that I had the flu. They never suspected what had led to my illness and I didn't know then the price I would have to pay for what I had done: I would never be able to have another child.

It was almost a week before I was well enough to leave my bed, and by then I was so horrified by what I had done, I couldn't look at the bottle again.

∞

For months, the bottle remained hidden. During that time, I would again be committed to the Goodna Mental Hospital. When I was finally released from there, I knew I had to bury my son because there was not a living soul I could entrust with my secret.

One night when I was home alone, I forced myself to climb into the cupboard and retrieve the bottle with its precious contents, which had haunted my dreams and me for two long years. I tried to remove the lid, but found it had rusted on. When I held the bottle up to the light, the tiny skeleton that floated near the top of the liquid hardly resembled the little boy I had named Ben.

Sadly, I took the bottle out into the garden, and there, at the base of a tree, I laid my son to rest – in a glass coffin.

That Same Year

I was at work at the house at nine o'clock on Monday evening, 22 May 1953, when Peg Connor called to me as I was taking a client down to my room.

'Jessie,' she said, using my working name, 'I want to see you when you come back.' And she smiled that brittle, cold smile that gave me goosebumps all over.

I nodded, unable to speak. A feeling of dread had clutched my heart. I instinctively knew there was something terribly wrong. It wasn't just Peg's dead smile – I was used to that – but for a brief instant I was looking at the mirthless grin of a death's head on her shoulders, before her face changed back again.

When I returned a short time later, Peg told me my mother was dead, and my father asked that I return home.

My mother had suffered a stroke and she was dead. And I didn't have a chance to say goodbye.

'It happened so quickly,' my father said when I reached home. 'She was sitting there singing and playing the piano when she suddenly held her head in her hands and cried, "*Oh, my head, the pain.*" Then she collapsed.'

The strange thing was that nobody could remember the song she had been playing.

How I regretted that my mother died while I was working in the place she hated so much. And worse – to be told of her death by that soulless woman, Peg Connor. Although my mother never said anything to me about what I was doing, I will never forget the look of sorrow in her eyes the night she found out I was back at the madam's.

∞

That night my father called me into his bedroom. When I went in, he was lying on his back staring at the ceiling, the covers drawn up to his chest.

'I don't want to be alone, Freddie,' he pleaded, tears glistening in his eyes. 'Will you come and sit with me for a while?'

I was surprised, though pleased, and thought how ironic it was that in his loneliest and saddest hour my father wanted to be with 'the sick and silly one', as he so often referred to me.

Nevertheless, I was deeply touched by his obvious pain. Besides, I didn't want to be alone either, so I stayed with him. I sat on the end of Mum's side of the bed and we talked into the small hours of the morning. We talked mostly about Mum and what a wonderful woman she was and how much we were going to miss her. We laughed at the funny things she used to say. Like, when she forgot things and had to go back for them: 'My legs will never save my head,' instead of the other way round. Or, 'Look, Roy, that car went around the corner on one leg,' instead of one wheel. We recalled how Mum had washed the clothes by hand and how painful it was for her when her hands were crippled with rheumatism, and Dad and the girls had done the washing for her.

Some time during the night I became cold and cramped, so while Dad was still talking (more to himself than to me) I crawled up the bed and slipped under the blankets and immediately fell asleep. I spent the rest of the night in my father's bed and for the first time in my life I wasn't afraid of him.

∞

The next morning I woke up with my father shaking me by the shoulder.

'Wake up, Freddie,' he said brightly, 'I've made us a nice cup of tea.'

I propped myself up and took the cup and saucer he held out to me. As he sat down on an old kitchen chair (where he always sat to put his shoes and socks on) and placed his own white enamel mug on the windowsill, I realised the sun was high in the sky. I had slept late. Dad had been up for hours, he said, and I noticed he had washed and shaved. The stubble of beard and the creases of pain of the night before had been ironed out, and those tortured eyes no longer haunted his face. His black hair slicked with Brylcreem showed the narrow, uniform furrows where the comb had been. He had changed out of his pyjamas into dark blue trousers and braces, blue flannelette shirt and an old grey cardigan that always smelled of tobacco. He wore the brown felt slippers that Mary had given him for his fifty-second birthday the year before.

The transformation was more remarkable because nothing had changed; my mother was still dead. The grief and pain still had to be borne, until time itself stepped in and applied the soothing balm of forgetfulness, allowing the healing to begin. Still, on this morning, my father was back in control and dealing with the most urgent of tasks. He had the ability to compartmentalise, relegating the non-essential tasks to the back of his mind, to be dealt with at a more appropriate time. I never knew him to have a too-hard basket.

That morning there was no sign of the debilitating grief of the previous evening. He talked now in a brisk, matter-of-fact manner, about the arrangements he must make for my mother's funeral. I was glad that I had in some small way helped him come to terms with his grief and enabled him to attend to the urgent business of laying my mother to rest.

Despite my father's self-control that morning, in the cold light of day as he talked about my mother's funeral the full realisation that she was dead plunged me into an emotional turmoil. I was nineteen, but I felt as if I were a little girl again. I felt a vital part of me had been torn out. I wanted to run to my mother for comfort, but I could never do that again. She was gone now forever.

Many Lifetimes

∞

Such a sense of loss I had not experienced before. Overwhelmed, I went horse riding. I don't know why, except that it somehow made me feel better. But my sisters saw this action as cold and callous behaviour.

'How could you go out, frivolously enjoying yourself when our mother has only just died?' The family thought it was an insult to our mother who was not yet buried.

These accusations hurt deeply, and made it even harder for me to come to terms with my grief. They made me feel guilty and worthless, a traitor to the memory of my mother.

Things may have been different had I had the support of my sisters. But sadly, we retreated into our own cubbyholes of pain. Each of us grieved in the same house together, yet in isolation. We simply didn't know how to love and support each other.

My cousin Lloyd Jackson came to our house, something he had never done before. We were not a close family and although Lloyd was the son of my mother's brother, Uncle James, I barely knew of his existence. He brought with him a young man who he introduced as Arnold Geoffrey Robinson. They were both in the National Service, and looked smart in their army uniforms.

At first, I assumed Lloyd had heard about my mother's death and had come to pay his respects. But when he asked why we were all crying, it became clear the visit was coincidental.

Lloyd and his friend did not stay long, but before they left Arnold said, 'I would like to see you again. Can I telephone you after the funeral?'

I hadn't really looked at Arnold until then. I saw that he was tall, with broad shoulders and slim hips. He had a tanned, rugged-looking face with blue eyes and black hair. When he smiled he had even, white teeth.

'Yes,' I replied listlessly, not even caring if he did or not, 'if you want to.' And I wrote down the telephone number.

My Mother's Funeral

On the morning of my mother's funeral I overheard Helen telling my father of a dream she had had the night before Mum died.

'I dreamt that I was standing at the front door when a large black mourning car pulled up at the front gate. Without a word Mum went past me down the stairs and walked towards the car. I saw a man dressed in black in the front seat and two nuns in black habits in the back seat. I was frightened and I called out to Mum not to get in the car, but she just turned and smiled at me, got in the car and sat between the two nuns. As the car started off, a Black and White taxi went slowly past the house.'

Even after Mum's death this seemed only a disturbing dream.

But then, due to some mix-up at the funeral home, a mourning car arrived to pick Dad up after he had already phoned for a taxi.

Helen stood at the front door and watched Dad open the door of the mourning car, and he turned and said, 'You and the girls take the taxi, Helen.' At that moment, a Black and White taxi cruised slowly past the house and, as the black car left, the taxi turned around and stopped at our gate.

Helen said she felt a chill pass over her body as she was reminded of her dream.

∞

I had never been to a funeral before, or a cremation, so I didn't know what to expect. When I went into the Albany Creek Crematorium, I saw a mobile trolley upon which rested my mother's coffin. It was closed.

I asked the funeral man – who came forward to offer his condolences – if I could see my mother. 'I'm sorry,' he said, 'but Mr May has requested that the coffin remain closed.'

Inside the chapel my sisters sat on long benches in front of a stage with closed, dark velvet curtains and I thought that the room looked more like a school concert hall than a place of mourning. I looked for my father, intending to ask him for just a few minutes with Mum, to see her so that I could say goodbye, but he was talking earnestly with the minister. Just then the organ music, which had been playing softly in the background, began to swell loudly to the tune of 'I'll Walk With God', or something like that, and the service began.

As I sat down in the front row the curtains slowly opened, revealing the coffin, now resting on a small dais. There was a small bunch of very pretty flowers on the coffin, from all the family.

I was still determined to see my mother just once more, before she was gone forever. It was more than simply wanting to say goodbye: although I had seen her coffin, it was difficult for me to believe the enormity of what this represented. I desperately needed to actually see and touch her dead body.

I sat restlessly while the minister's voice droned on and on, as he talked about my mother, Winifred Anne May, and her wonderful achievements. 'Winnie,' he said, 'was a wonderful woman.' How would he know? I thought to myself. He had never met her. 'A kind, caring person who stood staunchly beside her husband as they went through the many trials and tribulations of this life. Through bushfires, floods, sickness and the Great Depression, she was a loyal and faithful wife.' Oh, what a load of crap, I thought. I bet Dad put him up to this. What about the real Winifred, the creative woman? The artist, the poet, the singer and musician. In my mind, I again heard her playing the piano and I knew that was how I would always remember her. Not as a sad broken spirit, but a person who filled the world with the beauty of words and music.

'Let us pray,' the minister said. Dutifully, I bowed my head, closed my eyes and prayed that my mother would be rewarded in the next world for the kindness she had shown to every person, animal and living thing. But especially for her love and kindness to Peter and me. As the soft, muted sounds of the organ filled the chapel, I opened my eyes – and saw that my mother's coffin had disappeared.

The dais was empty.

I sat there stunned, even as my father stood up. 'C'mon, Freddie, it's all over, Mum's gone.'

I stared at him in disbelief and almost screamed. *At this very moment* flames were consuming my beautiful mother. This was the final betrayal. I could take no more. As my family began to file out of the chapel, I collapsed back into my seat and sobbed my heart out.

'C'mon, Freddie.' My father was standing beside me. 'I'll take you home.'

At that moment I didn't feel any emotion towards him. Neither pity nor anger, just a coldness that he had failed to care properly for my mother and now she was dead.

Perhaps this was why, after the funeral, I began to have nightmares about my mother being sealed up alive in a brick wall. Sometimes, too, I thought I could hear her playing the piano, just as I had heard her many times in the past.

Suddenly we were alone

My mother had been the buoy to which Peter and I had clung, neither of us able to survive on our own. Then, suddenly, she was gone and we were cast adrift. We could never have imagined how difficult our lives would be in the future.

My first thought after the funeral was about Peter. Up until then, my mother had taken care of the both of us. Now, suddenly and without warning, Peter and I were alone and, strangely, we barely knew each other. I was aware I wasn't capable of caring for Peter on my own, I couldn't even care for myself properly. I needed someone to help me, but who?

Four homeless girls

A week after the funeral, Arnold telephoned me and asked me to go to the pictures with him. I immediately gave up the paraldehyde, which I had been taking again ever since Goodna, so as not to be so odious to be near. I began drinking brandy instead. Brandy didn't have the medicinal qualities of paraldehyde, but it did help me sleep at night and deal with the depression.

After that first evening, Arnold and I saw each other on a regular basis.

But in July 1953, a few months after Mum died, Dad decided to sell up and head for the bush. My sisters and I met this news with mixed feelings. In one sense we wanted to be free of our father's tyranny, yet we were afraid of the world. We had never been given any instruction on survival skills, so we had no idea how to take care of ourselves. Now we had no choice in the matter.

When Diamond's secondhand dealer arrived at our house to give Dad an appraisal of what the furniture was worth, he was drunk as usual and accepted whatever paltry sum the dealer offered him. I was nineteen. Jan was fifteen, and Mary, who was the baby of the family, was eleven. Esmae, who was seventeen, was in Sydney. I don't know if the other girls discussed among themselves where they would go, but

I was not included. My father had always drummed into us that it was every man for himself; we were never taught any kind of sisterly love. 'It's a dog-eat-dog world out there,' he said, 'and you might as well learn that early in life.'

Almost silently, in a state of shock – compounded by grief – each one of us with our worldly possessions in a string bag slipped quietly out of the house – and into the four winds. When Esmae returned home from Sydney several months later, the house was deserted and desolate. She had no idea where the family had gone and she had no idea where to find us. Then, without any support from her family and no money, Esmae was forced to fend for herself. She must have felt so alone.

In the unfriendly environment of the city streets, I was soon returned to the mental hospital. And Peter began to stay in the different houses of my family.

Helen and me

Things were pretty bad for me in the hospital. I tried to be good so I wouldn't get into trouble and end up in the straitjacket or, worse, sent for shock treatment. But I felt lonely and unwanted. I cried a lot. I couldn't tolerate the uncertainty of my future. There didn't seem to be any end to my misery. My greatest fear was that my family would disown me because I was too much trouble. As it was, they couldn't understand why I had kept drinking brandy when, as my older sister Helen said, 'You know full well what the consequences will be.'

Released from the hospital, I tried once more, on a visit to Helen, to tell her how hopeless I felt. How there was an empty hole inside of me and I tried to fill it with alcohol. How I could not get through one day without suffering severe depression and how I couldn't cope with the everyday business of just living.

Finally I said, 'Helen, I don't drink because I like it. I drink because it is the only way I can get relief from depression.'

'That's silly,' Helen said. 'It's the drink that causes the depression.' Then she said, 'Well, maybe you are better off in the hospital. I can't help you any more. I have my own life to live too, you know, and if you are put back in the hospital then I won't have to help you any more. Anyway, why should I have the worry of your problems? You're a grown woman.'

I guess at that moment I died a little inside. Helen was my last hope and I saw it dashed before my eyes.

Helen got up from the kitchen table, stood at the sink, and began preparing vegetables for dinner. Without looking around she said, 'You had better go now, Audrey, Bob will be home soon and he said you had better not be here when he gets home.'

I was bitterly disappointed. I thought that for a moment my sister had understood the depth of my suffering. But she hadn't. Not that I blamed her – I didn't. If all the doctors in the mental hospital couldn't cure me or give me back some quality of life, then my sister, who already had a lot of problems herself, couldn't do any more than she had done. But I wished she had at least understood why I behaved the way I did.

So my plea for help went unheard because neither Helen nor I, nor any of my whole damn family, knew what was wrong with me or how to deal with it. There were many questions left unanswered, like: What is the matter with you? Why can't you control your drinking when the doctors say you're not an alcoholic? If you were, we could understand it. Alcoholism is a disease and people like our father and our brother John can't help themselves. So, why do you drink?

Sadly, I got to my feet and walked towards the front door. I didn't know where I was going. I had no money, and nowhere to live.

∞

I walked out of that door and up the street. I got to the corner, and had only just turned into Denman Street when a car pulled up beside me and the hairiest man I had ever seen leaned out of the car window and said, 'Can I give you a lift somewhere, luv?' I went over to the car and looked at him more closely. He had a dense thatch of long black hair. He didn't have a shirt on, and his neck, chest, shoulders and arms were covered with thick, downy black hair. I noticed his eyes then. Usually I look into a person's eyes first, but the expanse of hair on this huge body fascinated me. He had large brown eyes with a broad nose that dominated his large brown face. He was smiling broadly too, showing a double row of gleaming white teeth. I liked him and took the ride.

We only knew each other for that short journey, but right from the start of it we got on famously. He introduced himself as Harry. 'That's me,' he said, 'happy-go-lucky

Harry,' and guffawed loudly. I noticed then that he was wearing long black trousers.

'I'm just on my way to visit the missus,' he confided, 'she's just had another little 'un.'

I didn't like his chances of getting into the hospital without a shirt. But he must have read my mind, because just then he reached over and flipped the glove box open, and drew out a T-shirt, neatly folded.

'Mussen forget to put me shirt on.' Harry laughed. 'I remember when the first little 'un was born. I was so excited I rushed into the ward with just an old pair of shorts, no shirt. Well Jesus, didn't the missus give it to me.'

By the time we got into Brisbane I was laughing along with Harry; his cheerfulness was infectious, and for a while I was able just to enjoy a little friendly humour.

August 1953

Marriage to Arnold, aged 19

When Arnold returned to Brisbane and asked me to marry him, I was pleased. Not excited or ecstatic, but happy and relieved. Still, I was aware of a niggling doubt that things were happening too fast. My instinct told me to wait. 'You don't know this person,' it said, 'how do you know he is the right man for you? The right father for Peter?' 'I don't know,' I answered back irritably, 'how does anyone know for sure?' And so my thoughts went back and forth. Finally, my need to love and be loved overrode my reservations, and I said, 'Yes, Arnold, I will marry you.'

While the details were being finalised I asked my brother Rod if he thought I was doing the right thing.

'Bloody hell, Freddie,' he yelled at me. 'You've already told the bloke you'll marry him, bit late to back out now. Besides, you orta think yourself lucky he wants to marry you at all, not too many blokes would take a kid that wasn't his.'

I knew Rod was right. I really should be thankful that somebody would have me and Peter. Yes. My mind was made up. I would marry Arnold. I went to McDonnell and East and bought some white lace to make my wedding dress. My sister-in-law Annie (Rod's wife) had a sewing machine and I asked her if she would help me make my dress.

Annie was a tall, gaunt woman about my age, but old beyond her years. She was painfully thin and had three children.

Annie was only too happy to help me make my dress, but when I showed her the white lace material, she staggered back.

'You can't wear white!' she gasped. 'You're not a virgin, and worse, you already have a child!'

'But Annie,' I argued, 'my mother was married in a white wedding dress and she had two children, Robert and Beryl. And,' I argued further, 'that was in the 1920s.'

'Yes,' Annie said, 'but remember, that was in the Roaring Twenties when young people could do pretty much as they liked. You won't get away with it today. Why, if people found out, they would crucify you. Maybe even say you aren't properly married.'

'Oh.' I was quite dismayed. 'But no one will know, you and Rod are my witnesses and will be the only ones there.'

'God will know,' Annie said ominously.

'Stuff God!' I burst out angrily. 'He has no right to stop me from being a real bride.' And I dissolved into tears.

'Then you can't get married,' Annie said. At that time we knew nothing about a civil marriage ceremony, it was a church or nothing.

'What about a pink dress?' Annie suggested more kindly.

'But I don't have enough money to buy any more material,' I sobbed.

'Well,' Annie offered, 'I'll buy the pink lace for you, and I'll keep the white lace in return, okay?'

∞

Ever since I was a young girl I had dreamed of being married in a beautiful white wedding dress and walking down the aisle of a magnificent cathedral crowded with people. But apparently I had committed some sort of dreadful crime and my punishment was to be a second-rate bride. I was glad my mother was not there to see my shame. I was so bitterly disappointed.

On 18 August 1953, Arnold and I were married in St John's Presbyterian Church in the inner-city suburb of Annerley. In the small, silent, empty church I walked dismally down the aisle in a garish pink lace dress. My brother and his wife were witnesses, Annie resplendent in my white lace.

∞

Arnold had arranged for us to stay with friends of his, somewhere near Ipswich, after the wedding. We went there by train. I can't remember the name of the station or who his friends were, but Arnold said they were putting on a keg for us and I imagined this was to be our wedding reception.

When we arrived most of the people were already drunk. There was a lot of noise, swearing and arguing going on in the house. I hated it and, after a couple of hours, when I managed to get Arnold on his own I asked him if we might leave and find a place of our own. He exploded.

'What's the matter, aren't my friends good enough for you?' He slapped me across the face, first with his open hand and then with the back of his hand.

Peter screamed and ran to me. But Arnold grabbed him and threw him to the floor.

I picked Peter up in my arms and ran to our bedroom, opened the door and pulled it shut behind me. I looked for something to barricade it with but all the furniture was old solid-cedar wood, and I couldn't move it. So I propped a wooden chair under the door handle, hoping it would delay Arnold long enough for us to escape.

I went to the window and saw that the bedroom, unlike the front of the house which was quite high, was only a few feet off the ground. Frantically, I grabbed my port and tossed it out of the window. I climbed out and jumped to the ground. Without further prompting Peter jumped into my arms. But I was still off balance and we both went sprawling in a flurry of arms and legs in the dirt.

Quickly, driven by fear of discovery, I regained my feet and clutched Peter's hand in one of mine and the port in the other. We ran without stopping the half-mile or so to the railway station. I was too frightened to wait on the lit railway platform as I knew it was the first place Arnold would look for us, so we hid in some low bushes across the tracks, ready to run back to the station at the first glimpse of the train's headlight coming around the bend.

I don't know how long it was before the train came, but it was an agonising wait. Peter and I huddled together, not only for warmth but also to gain strength from each other. As we waited, I wondered how long it would be before Arnold came to the bedroom door and found it barricaded. I was counting on this to buy us a little time and increase our chances of getting away. Then I remembered something that sent my heart plunging down into the pit of my stomach.

When I had fled with Peter in my arms into the bedroom, I'd pulled the door shut behind me – *behind me!* The door opened outwards. The chair was useless.

Just then, in the eerie silence as the cold westerly wind dropped momentarily, I heard the train and it appeared around the bend. I grabbed Peter in my arms and just managed to cross the tracks before it reached the platform.

∞

Peter and I got off the train at Darra and walked to Helen's place.

I told her what had happened.

She was unsympathetic and said, 'God! If you're going to run away every time you get a smack in the mouth you'll never get a man.'

I asked if Peter and I could stay with her until I found a job.

'All right, but remember you're a married woman now and nobody's responsibility but your husband's. You'd better go back and apologise to Arnold in the morning because you can't stay here too long.'

I had been sure she would understand. But she didn't.

We had grown up in a home with drinking and violence and Helen felt it was a wife's duty to stay with her husband, no matter what the circumstances were. Just as my mother had done and her mother before her. But I was damned if I would. I thought every person, no matter who they were, had a right to be treated fairly and decently, and I would not go back.

24 December 1953

My brother John

My brother John was three years older than me and had suffered rejection all his life. As a baby he almost died from infantile paralysis — a disease which caused him brain damage — and although John survived he was left retarded. Then, at about eight years old, when crossing a busy highway with Patrick — who was only one year older — John was hit by a car and suffered severe head injuries.

Patrick had to drag John off the road by the feet before someone else hit him. No one knows why he didn't hear the car. Patrick believes that the straw hat John was wearing caused the accident because it had a torn brim that hung down in front of his face. On the other hand I recall Mum saying that John was blind in one eye from the disease he had. Such are the vagaries of memory.

What disadvantaged John further was his great size. He

was well over six feet tall, had enormous broad shoulders and was so badly coordinated that he shuffled when he walked. Out of all of Mum's children John was the one who looked the most Aboriginal. He couldn't hide it as the rest of us could. His skin was very dark and, with a broad, flattened nose, his features showed none of the European influence.

All his life John had been the brunt of cruel jokes. He used to speak in a slow drawl and his movements were also slow and clumsy. It wasn't hard for people to see he was retarded. He became an alcoholic at a young age and he was forever being picked up by the police for being drunk.

John was a very angry young man. He would get into fights after being deliberately provoked and, because of his great size, police would use unnecessary force to restrain him. John often came home the next day bruised and battered, with clothes torn and dirty. Even though alcohol got him into constant trouble, it was the only relief, however temporary, he could find from the neglect, cruelty and loneliness of a hybrid Aboriginal, a social outcast. In many ways he was a gentle, childlike creature. Trusting, forgiving and always trying to please. He used to talk about his pipe-dreams of one day being rich, saying 'Then people couldn't kick me around and make me apologise for things I didn't do.' I knew what John meant. I had heard my brothers talking about how people used to set John up and leave him to take the blame. He often talked about how he would like to live in the bush and live off the land just as the traditional Aboriginals used to do. John had this endearing way of tilting his head to one side and saying, 'Do you think I could, Freddie? Do you think I could? Really?'

Yet John suffered uncontrollable rages and fits of depression, as I did. I know there was not one person in our family who did not pity him and feel deeply the sadness of his affliction. Nevertheless he was ostracised even from his relations and friends, because he wasn't normal and they were ashamed of him.

Years later when I read John Steinbeck's novel *Of Mice and Men*, I could liken John to the childlike character Lennie. Lennie and John both led a dog's life. How I wished John had had a minder like George. And yes, perhaps dying the same way with a bullet through the brain would have been better for John, instead of the way he actually did die.

John and me

By the time I was twenty and John was twenty-three, I had been in psychiatric and mental hospitals on and off since I was fourteen. No member of my family wanted to have me around any more. I was back in hospital again and, legally, I could not be released unless someone agreed to be responsible for me.

It was on 24 December 1953 (our mother had been dead seven months) that the doctor told me my brother John, who I had not seen for several years, had applied to have me released in his custody for twenty-eight days. As I waited eagerly for my brother to come and pick me up, I fantasised that John and I would go away, just the two of us, and live out our lives in a wilderness, away from people, alcohol and the pain of being social outcasts.

Then, suddenly, John was there beside me.

I saw people staring at John, but what did I care? What did it matter if his clothes were old and tattered, if in place of a belt there was a piece of rope tied around his waist, holding his trousers up? He was someone who cared enough to come and take me home, and I loved him.

As we left I was excited and bubbling over with questions. 'Where have you been, John? How did you know where I was? Who told you?'

'Hey, hang on, one question at a time,' John said. 'I called in to see Helen and she told me you were in the hospital. She sure don't think much of you, Freddie, said she wouldn't get you out again, no way. So I said, "We can't just leave Freddie there." So here I am.'

'But where have you been, John? You have been gone so long and I was worried about you.' I couldn't even remember how long it had been.

'Aw, you don't have to worry about me, Freddie,' John said, slightly abashed. 'I've been down south doing a bit of work here and there, enough to keep me going.'

As we reached the corner of the main road, John stopped and said, 'Well, Freddie, this is where I leave you, you'll be right now, okay?'

'Leave me?' I repeated stupidly. 'Why, John? Where are you going? Can't I come with you?'

'Sorry, love,' he replied. 'I'm staying at a mate's place.'

I knew this wasn't true. For one thing, John didn't have any mates. Yet I also knew he wasn't capable of making up a story as he quickly forgot what he had just said.

I believe the truth was that John was barely able to look after himself, let alone me, and that he was probably living with those riverbank blacks again. I remembered before Mum died, how she worried about John living with the blacks. 'They live dangerously,' she'd said, 'drinking methylated spirits mixed with cheap plonk. It will kill them all one day.' But John had found forgiveness, kindness and acceptance in the Aboriginal community. It was where he wanted to be.

I was almost about to bust out bawling as I watched my brother walk away. I ran after him, calling, 'John, John, wait!' He turned around, but I could see that he had no idea how frightened I was to be left alone. He thought all I wanted was to get out of the hospital, and he had helped me do that. What more did I want?

'Have you got any money, John?' I asked timidly.

'Sorry, love,' he replied, with genuine regret in his voice. 'I've only got a return ticket. Anyway, Freddie, you know I don't ever have any money.' With that he turned towards the railway station. I knew this was true but still I was devastated. I had no money, not even train fare.

∞

I walked towards the main road, intending to hitch a ride into the city.

It wasn't long before a car carrying some high-spirited drunken teenagers stopped and asked where I was going. When I said I wanted to go to the city, the driver, a fresh-faced kid with an Elvis Presley haircut and who looked no more than sixteen, said, 'Hop in, the more the merrier.' I was glad he thought so because there were already three young girls in the back seat, and I barely managed to squash in beside them.

The car took off before I had the door properly shut.

When we reached the city I got out in Adelaide Street, the car sped off and I made my way down to Anzac Square. As I sat under the shade of a tree watching the pigeons cooing and fighting, I wished I had some breadcrumbs to feed them, and that reminded me how hungry I was, and then I wished I had a loaf of bread for myself.

I sat there for the best part of two hours, watching the crowds of people doing last-minute Christmas shopping, amusing myself by trying to guess what their packages might contain.

As the shadows grew long on the ground, I made my way down into Edward Street, then right into Queen Street, and walked the few yards to the Grand Central Hotel. In a matter of minutes, there was a young man asking if he could buy me a drink. I would rather have had something to eat, but I settled for potato crisps and peanuts.

The night was young as we drank our beer and ate the nuts. He introduced himself as Todd and told me about his girlfriend who had broken off their engagement because she was pregnant to another man. I listened sympathetically, but couldn't help thinking that if that was all he had to worry about he was well off. Several times he asked why I was drinking alone, but I sidestepped the question. I didn't want to talk about myself for fear of becoming morbid – when you start crying into your beer nobody wants to know you.

After a while he said, 'Would you care to come to my place for dinner?'

I thought he would never ask. I was starving. So when he had picked up some beer, a couple of pieces of fish and a double serving of chips, Todd hailed a taxi and we went to West End.

His flat was a typical bachelor's quarters. Unwashed dishes in the sink, clothes draped over every chair, shoes, socks and newspapers all over the floor. The clothes, however, were quickly gathered up and shoved into a cane laundry basket.

We ate the fish and chips from the newspaper they came in. 'Less washing up,' Todd explained, but I guessed that perhaps there were no clean dishes.

After we had consumed the rest of the beer, Todd casually said, 'It's late, what say we turn in?'

'Yes,' I replied. 'It's been a long day.'

We went to bed. We made love – well, he did, a few seconds before he fell asleep. I thought how lucky his girlfriend was . . . and then I was sound asleep.

In the morning Todd was up and gone before I awoke. There was a five-pound note on the table and a scrawled message: *Merry Christmas, just pull the door shut when you leave.* The note was unsigned.

I helped myself to a cup of tea, then washed up the dishes in the sink. I was about to leave when, as an afterthought, I picked up the pen and wrote *Thanks* at the bottom of the note. I pulled the door shut and headed downtown.

∞

Since it was Christmas Day there were no pubs open, and the only place I knew I could get a drink was at the sly grog shop at South Brisbane. I walked up Melbourne Street towards the city, turned into a side street and saw a man hiding in a doorway. He was known as a 'cockatoo' – he would warn the sly grog sellers when any police were approaching. When I turned down the next alleyway there was a queue of people waiting at the closed window of a dilapidated building.

Suddenly the wooden shutters were thrown open, several cartons of beer were handed over and the whole queue of people followed the cartons back onto the street.

As they passed me, one of the boys said, 'Wanna go to a party?' I said yes, but where was it? 'Jus folla us,' he said, obviously already very drunk.

We went a short way down Melbourne Street, the cartons borne aloft on strong shoulders, followed by a motley crew of seasoned drinkers. Finally we got to an old house bulging with people. Somebody was playing a guitar and in the rear of the house I could hear someone trying to knock out a tune on a harmonica. It was obvious that all this had been going on since the previous night.

The man who had invited me to the party handed me a paper cup and filled it with beer, saying, 'Yer don't wanna drink from them glasses, dearie, gins have been drinking outa them.'

I don't know how much time had passed when I became aware of a lot of noise outside on the footpath – shouting, swearing and the sound of bodies hitting the ground. An old fellow passed through the room at a fast trot. Without stopping he said to me, 'Run, luv, the cops are here.'

When I tried to get up I found that there was something wrong with my legs. I couldn't seem to stand. Next minute

I was raised in the air, my legs dangling helplessly above the ground, as two burly policemen, one on each side, carried me out to the kerbside.

Then we were all bundled into the waiting paddy wagons and taken to the South Brisbane watch-house.

From there I was taken to the Brisbane General Hospital, where I was given an injection and transferred by ambulance back to Goodna Mental Hospital, which I had left with my brother John just under twenty-four hours before. It was Christmas Day, 1953.

1954, Aged 20

Working on a sheep station

When next I was released from the hospital, in the care of my father, I realised that the blackouts and periods of disorientation were becoming more frequent and lasting longer. I couldn't even look after Peter properly and he was often with Mary, or living with others in the family. Besides, I thought that during one of these blackouts I might lose control of my mind and recede into the world of the insane. I was terribly afraid of this happening. I knew I wasn't mad like some of the inmates at the hospital – I was lucid enough to make the comparison, otherwise I might never have known the difference!

I had to get out of the city. I knew that it was the drinking and the mental hospital that were tearing me apart. So I placed Peter in the Blackheath Orphanage where my sister Jan worked as a housemaid. Then I went to the Town and

Country employment agency, in Queen Street, and registered as a housemaid or laundress.

A few days later, I got a job on a sheep station at Nobby, a small town between Toowoomba and Warwick. I would travel there by train, my fare paid by my employer, Mrs Bulfin. She had arranged for the money to be deducted from my first pay cheque.

At first, I was excited about the job. But once I was on the train, I became very worried: I had had many jobs before and I could never keep them. Not since my mother died and we all left the family home at Seven Hills had I been able to stay in a job for more than a few months. Could I control my rages, crying fits and moments of disorientation? I didn't know, but I was determined to try.

∞

When the train pulled into Nobby railway station, a middle-aged lady came towards me, hand outstretched. 'Hello, Audrey?' Smiling broadly then, she said, 'I'm Mrs Bulfin.' I hadn't expected that. I had simply been told I would be met at the station, and I thought she would have sent a station hand to pick me up.

I smiled a little uncertainly and nodded, and we shook hands.

Mrs Bulfin looked like a schoolteacher, which made me inwardly shudder. She was of medium height and build and her thin brown hair was cut short in a style we used to know as the 'saucepan cut' because a saucepan was placed on a child's head and the hair was cut level with the rim. Her face had an unhealthy grey pallor, and behind her gold-rimmed glasses her eyes were grey and misty. She had a small, pinched nose that also seemed watery. She alternately dabbed at the corners of her eyes and the edge of her nostrils with a delicately perfumed white handkerchief. I had always liked to see ladies with white handkerchiefs, they always seemed so feminine. Mrs Bulfin was anything but the robust suntanned countrywoman I had known in my childhood.

When we reached the homestead it was not the big sprawling old Queenslander of the western stations, but a compact, moderate house common to most Brisbane suburbs.

My room was small, yet adequately furnished and quite homely, I thought. I unpacked my port, hung my few dresses in the wardrobe, and packed away the rest in the chest of drawers.

Then I returned to the kitchen to begin work.

∞

I loved being out on the station and my health improved greatly. I rarely felt alone and frightened as I did in the city, because the other station workers included me in all of their sporting and social activities. We often went fishing or swimming in the river on Saturday afternoon. They mostly hunted wild pigs with a pack of dogs. Other times we went out in the night, spotlighting kangaroos. I always felt sorry for the roos; they seemed so defenceless against rifles and dogs.

On Saturday nights, though, I declined to join the others when they went out on the town. I wasn't able to cope with the drinking and meeting strangers yet.

I liked working for Mrs Bulfin. The work was light and there was more free time than I had ever known in any other job. Any day after lunch I was allowed to ride Mrs Bulfin's mare, Lilac, so-called because of her colour. She was the prettiest and daintiest horse I had ever seen, and ever so comfortable to ride. Mrs Bulfin had trained her herself.

'I don't ride any more these days,' Mrs Bulfin said. 'Maybe I will again, maybe later.'

But Mrs Bulfin never did ride again.

The following winter she died suddenly of pneumonia. I was devastated. Other members of the family took over the management of the house and property.

My services were no longer required so I returned to Brisbane.

Into 1955

Returning to Drake Street

I wandered around the streets unable to settle down. The death of Mrs Bulfin weighed heavily upon my mind. She had been one of the very few people I had allowed to befriend me. Although it sounds childish now, I somehow felt betrayed, like she had no right to die.

Late in 1954 I returned to the house in Drake Street. I was a lot tougher now and not so easily frightened. Soon after I started back at work there, perhaps only a matter of weeks, there was a violent thunderstorm. The house was lashed with huge pellets of rain which hit the tin roof with such velocity that, from within, it sounded like the rat-tat-tat of rapid machine-gun fire. The noise was deafening; you could hardly hear yourself speak. Outside, the howling wind raged and assaulted the ancient house so violently it threatened to dislodge it from its stumps.

Lightning bolts cracked loudly, then sizzled and crackled like tinfoil.

The lightning flashes that lit the sky that night resembled the network of blue veins across an old person's face. This awesome display of nature's absolute power left no doubt in my mind that something was really in charge of this planet.

At the height of the storm, as I opened the wire gate at the top of the stairs to let a client out – quickly closing it against the men queuing on the stairs – a face suddenly appeared pressed against the wire, fingers curled around the fencing chain-wire of the gate.

I ignored the man, but as I turned away I heard him say in a loud stage whisper, 'Audrey, wait.'

I stopped dead in my tracks. I didn't recognise the voice, but he had called me Audrey, and I was only ever known here by my pseudonym, Jessie. This had to be someone who knew me from my natural world, not the surreal world of the Drake Street house.

Fearfully, I turned and looked into the face of the young man. I still didn't recognise him. He looked slightly ridiculous with his dark hair plastered flat on his head. There were raindrops hanging from his eyebrows and lashes. And in one hand he was clutching a Stetson cowboy hat.

'Audrey! It's me, Arnold, can we talk for a minute?'

I was immobilised with shock and disbelief. I wanted to shove his hat down his throat to shut him up. But without a word I opened the gate and let him in. As I led him silently to my room, thoughts were racing through my head so fast they were tumbling over each other. How did he know where to find me? It wasn't coincidence, Arnold had never paid for sex in his life. He openly boasted that he just took sex whenever and from whomever he pleased. *Helen*, I thought bitterly – she always did have a soft spot for Arnold.

I closed the bedroom door. 'What do you want?'

'I want you to come back to me,' he said, looking very much like a hurt little boy with his hat in his hand, head bowed slightly.

But I wasn't fooled, I had seen how quickly men like Arnold could be galvanised into anger and violence. I listened to his regrets and apologies for his past actions.

'I love you both so very much,' he said then. 'It was the drink, I promise I won't drink any more.'

I wasn't really deceived by what Arnold was saying, I had heard it all before, from my father. The excuses, remorse and promises, these were simply words to curry favour. They didn't mean a damn thing. But oh, how I wished they were true.

Arnold was talking excitedly now. 'I have this really good job to go to and I want you to come with me.'

'Really, what sort of job?' I asked.

'Fencing on a cattle station!'

'Where?' I was becoming more curious.

'Out west, near a little town called Betoota.'

Now I was interested.

I remembered the bush of my childhood in Charleville – the flowers like the kangaroo paw, which mimicked the kangaroo with its lifelike resemblance; the goanna, which stands perfectly still and is easily mistaken for a dead branch; the shy grey koalas sleeping in the treetops; the fat wombat, busily searching for food; the beautiful dingo which, though much maligned, helps keep the balance of nature. This was the bush John and I always dreamed of ... the place where we could escape the cruelty of people and the soul-destroying alcohol. And now Arnold was offering all of this to me.

I couldn't refuse.

We left on the Western Mail train a few days later.

Twenty-One Years Old

The train trip

The train trip was fun for Peter, and I enjoyed passing through the Queensland bush that I loved so much. I named trees and flowers that I was familiar with and Peter laughed delightfully when he saw families of emu running and kangaroos bounding away as the noise of the train startled them. But all too soon it was over.

We left the train at Quilpie, and began the long trek by mail-truck, first to Windorah, and then on to Betoota. As we travelled, I noticed that the landscape was changing from a green bushland to a flat, sparse, red, desert-like country, which became more desolate the further inland we went.

We stayed overnight in Windorah. Arnold got very drunk and an argument developed between us on the street, with Peter watching. Arnold punched me in the face, breaking my false teeth.

My mouth was cut and bleeding as I ran to our room in the hotel. Arnold followed me and, when I threatened to leave him, he took a large knife and slashed all my clothes.

That night, Arnold stayed downstairs.

By morning, he was sober and extremely apologetic. He came begging my forgiveness, blaming it on the alcohol. I knew in my heart that I shouldn't travel further with him, I knew I should turn around and go back home.

But I didn't have a home, and I had nothing to return to. So, sadly, Peter and I boarded the mail-truck again with Arnold, and travelled on to Betoota. When we arrived, our gear was transferred to a station truck and we were taken out to the campsite.

Arriving at the campsite

As our tent and belongings were unloaded from the truck, I looked in bitter dismay at the isolation and barrenness of the place that was to be our home. There was red sand that stretched for miles. Sparse and stunted vegetation dotted the landscape and, apart from a scavenger bird circling in the distance, not a living creature was to be seen. As I watched the truck drive off, tears came to my eyes – I was now alone somewhere 'out west' with a small child and a violent man I hardly knew.

When I had agreed to accompany Arnold to his new job – fencing on a cattle station – I had imagined that we would be living in the bush. The bush I had known in my childhood in Charleville and Mitchell. The bush John and I had dreamed of. A land of tall gums and scented trees, of wildflowers, birds and bush creatures. Not this silent desert, where the blistering heat seared the skin and burnt it black. Here the moisture was sucked from your body until your throat was parched and dry and your dehydrated skin wrinkled and aged prematurely. Worst of all was the deafening silence, broken only at night by the mournful cry of a dingo.

Out here it was easy to believe that we were the only people left on earth. We had no telephone or wireless. Country Queensland didn't even have television. I had no calendar. The days, the weeks and months, stretched into an interminable timelessness. It was as if we were caught in a time warp without a past or future. Words like *next year* had no meaning. Nothing did, except the here and now and the struggle to survive.

I believe I survived because I lived one day at a time. And when I was later asked how long we camped there, I had to say I didn't know. But later I remembered that I had had three menstrual cycles so we must have been there at least three months.

The dingoes

Peter was only five years old and he could not bear to watch his mother being brutalised, so he would slip quietly out of the tent and disappear. Afterwards I would find him in the dry creek-bed playing in the sand.

It was on one such occasion that I found him with a litter of four dingo pups. As I approached I could hear Peter laughing, amid strange yelping sounds. Then I saw him, happier than he had been since we arrived at the campsite. He was rolling over and over in the sand, laughing deliciously as the pups pulled at his clothes, his feet, his hair. I savoured the scene. But only for a moment – those dingo pups were wild and their mother would be nearby and could be dangerous.

It was then that I saw her.

She was sitting on the opposite bank, about twenty feet away, apparently unperturbed that her pups were with a child. But I knew dingoes were unpredictable at the best of times and I knew a hungry dingo with a litter of pups was a positive threat.

The mother seemed to sense that Peter posed no danger to her or the pups; but I was a different matter. I dared not go any closer.

I watched as the late afternoon sunlight filtered through the leaves and played upon her yellow, lustreless coat, which hung on her skinny frame like ill-fitting clothes. She blended with the autumn shades of the ochre and brown countryside. She was in extremely poor condition, due no doubt to rearing a family in this dry, desolate land.

Quietly I called to my son, 'Peter, say goodbye to the pups now, it's time to go home.' He turned to look at me, still laughing and holding up a pup by its two front legs for me to see. I groaned inwardly but said in the same careful monotone, 'Peter, put the puppy down gently and walk slowly towards me.'

For once, he obeyed me without further argument. It was as if he could sense the importance of my words although he himself did not feel threatened.

As Peter started to walk away, the pups began to follow him. The mother suddenly got to her feet and leapt lightly into the creek-bed with him.

Now I knew real fear.

In my mind's eye, I saw the dingo fly at Peter's throat and tear him apart. In the same instant, I seemed to see another son, lying at my feet in a pool of blood. The image destroyed my last vestige of self-control.

I tried to scream out to Peter to run, but all that came out was a rasping cough. I stood there like a piece of petrified wood, while he turned and waved goodbye to the puppies, who had, for a short while, given him so much pleasure.

Warily, the mother stopped a short distance from Peter. Then, crooning softly deep in her throat, she called to her pups, and they all trotted away up the creek.

∞

There was no one to talk to out there, except Peter. My husband rarely if ever spoke to me, other than to scream obscenities into my face. At these times, he would force my arm up my back, jerking it up painfully until I thought it would break. He shoved his face into mine so close his stale hot breath would sting my face. I tried to turn away – only to have him squeeze my cheeks in his huge hand and force me to look at him.

How I wished I could die. Just wake up one morning and be dead. How I wished *he* would die.

Peter and I were alone and helpless and Arnold vented his anger upon us at will. All pretence was gone. Arnold was a sadist who simply enjoyed hurting someone smaller and weaker than himself. Daily he would bash and rape me, battering my face until I could scarcely see out of my eyes. I knew he was going to kill Peter and me eventually, and get away with it too – I hadn't seen any of my family before I left, so nobody knew where we had gone, nobody would miss us anyway. There was no one to turn to and nowhere to run.

Here in this no-man's-land we were imprisoned as surely as if we were surrounded by high walls and barbed wire. We were imprisoned by the tyranny of distance, by the killing heat, by the endless miles of burning red sand and by our own fear. If we attempted to escape, we would be killed by the elements, and if we stayed we would be killed by my husband.

That was when I decided I had to do something. I decided to kill Arnold.

∞

A few days after I'd decided, Arnold made his first big mistake. Up until then he had kept his rifles locked safely away in a long tin box with a strong padlock. On this day Arnold unlocked the box, took out two of the rifles and handed one to me.

The disbelief almost showed on my face.

He looked at me quickly, but then said, 'Can you shoot?'

'Yes,' I said. I had learned to shoot with my brother Rod. He had a .44 pump-action Remington and had let me have a go when he was target-shooting at old bottles and cans.

'We're going after those dingoes that have been howling every night. They sound real close,' Arnold said.

As I lifted the tent-flap to follow him, I looked back at Peter.

'I won't be long,' I said.

Peter nodded silently and went on playing with some sticks and bits of string. Very soon after we arrived he had learned not to cry or complain when Arnold was around. Like the dingo pups he played with, he had understood that there were times when he had to be quiet or take the consequences; the mother dingo, too, would kill a noisy pup if she could not silence it, rather than let it attract predators to her den.

As I followed Arnold up the creek-bed, I raised the rifle and aimed at the back of his head.

But I just couldn't pull the trigger.

I couldn't murder him in cold blood.

The Fence-Line

The fence Arnold was building was outlined against the horizon about a mile from the campsite. Sometimes the fence appeared to turn into a caravan of camels strung together in single file. Sometimes they were walking on the ground but other times they appeared to be travelling above it. As I watched, I saw Arnold's figure separate from the fence and turn towards the campsite, his torso and limbs distorted. To me he resembled a praying mantis or a stick creature growing larger the nearer he approached.

I don't know how much of this distortion was generated by my abject terror of this man or, as I have learned since, by the heat waves and mirages common in the desert. I feared I was losing my mind, but I knew that for Peter's sake I must hang on to my sanity as long as I was able.

February 1956, Aged 22

King Cole

This was my frame of mind when one day I saw a dust cloud rolling across the desert. At first I thought it was another illusion. Dust storms were common out here, but they didn't roll along in a small ball as this one was doing.

I watched intently as the cloud came closer, until it turned into a large truck.

It stopped at our tent and a tall stranger, his skin burnt almost black by the sun, jumped down. As he strode towards me I saw he was about fifty years old with grey eyes above a slightly crooked nose. I guessed he was no stranger to violence. Yet, as he looked at my battered and bloodied face, a look of disbelief and horror passed across his face.

'What happened to you?' he asked in amazement, though I could see, in his steely eyes and the hard set of his chin, that he already knew.

I didn't answer him straight away, but fearfully looked past him towards the fence. Arnold was approaching at a fast trot.

The stranger followed my gaze.

'Who's that?' he asked grimly.

Quickly, before I started crying, I told him how Arnold had physically abused Peter and me, and we had no way of getting away.

'Well, nobody has to put up with that kind of treatment. Be ready at nine o'clock in the morning. Bring only what you can carry and I'll get you out of here.'

He warned me not to attempt to pack anything at all; if Arnold found out, the rescue attempt would have to be abandoned. 'Then,' he said, 'I believe you would be in extreme danger.' He did not add 'and so would I', but we both knew how dangerous Arnold was and that he would not hesitate to shoot us all and leave our bones bleaching in the desert sun.

There was no time for more because, at that moment, Arnold arrived and the stranger went forward to greet him.

'G'day,' he said in a typical bushman's drawl, 'I'm King Cole, well-borer. I'm camped a few miles over yonder.' He nodded in the direction from which he had come. 'I was just telling your missus that I didn't know you were here. The manager asked the other night if I had made your acquaintance yet – and that is the first I'd heard that you were even here. I thought you and your missus might like to come over and have a beer some time.'

Later, after King had gone, Arnold suspiciously questioned me about what I had said.

'Nothing. I told him nothing.'

Arnold didn't believe me. He kept questioning me and eventually smacked me around a bit, but not hard this time. No doubt he was wary of damaging me any further, because now there was a witness.

Our dash for freedom

The next morning Arnold didn't leave at his usual time, but hung around the camp long after sunup. I was afraid that he wasn't going to leave the camp at all that day. However, after about two hours, without a word to me, he picked up his waterbag and started walking towards the fence.

King's words were still ringing in my ears – *Be ready at nine o'clock* – but I had no way of knowing the time except by the position of the sun. My watch had been lost during the fight at Windorah. All I could do was keep a lookout for the first telltale sign of the small dust cloud I had seen the day before.

When at last I saw it, my mind couldn't grasp the enormity of what was happening. Peter and I huddled together until the truck pulled up at the flap of the tent. King jumped down and in one swoop he threw Peter into the cabin and me after him. I couldn't believe it – we were finally escaping from my husband and all the horror we had been through. We had no money and no possessions, just the clothes we were wearing and Peter's little school port, where I had hidden our photographs from Arnold.

As we roared off in the direction the truck had come from, I looked back across the plain and saw the figure of

Arnold running from the fence – but he was too late, we were speeding away, long gone to safety and freedom.

∞

King drove to the station airstrip. There the three of us were the only people to board a small light plane to Winton, where we were transferred onto a larger plane bound for Brisbane.

It was on the second plane that people stared at me curiously. I knew my face was a mess, but I didn't know how bad it really was. To make matters worse, the beating Arnold had given me the night before had opened up old wounds.

Gingerly I put my fingers to my face and tried to imagine what it looked like. The most I could determine by touch was that both my eyes were badly swollen, as were my lips. I couldn't see very well. They felt enormous, and I had to continually dab lightly at my left eyebrow, which was again split open and weeping a yellowish fluid that was not blood. I had no upper dentures. Those were smashed when Arnold had hit me in the mouth before we even arrived at the camp.

That had been my chance to escape, and I missed it.

As the plane rose high in the air I saw the huge expanse of the great Australian outback which had imprisoned us for three months – was it only three months? Only then did I feel some of the tension ease from my body.

Up until that moment I think I had fully expected Arnold to appear and forcibly drag us from the plane and take us back to the camp of horrors. I couldn't believe that a complete stranger like King Cole would go to the expense and trouble of rescuing another man's wife and child. It seemed somehow un-Australian to interfere in domestic violence. Nobody came to my mother's aid when she screamed for help. Neighbours would ignore it. And when we heard other women being bashed by their husbands, Dad would say, 'Stay out of it, it's nothing to do with you.' That's why what King did for us was so wonderful. He was willing to risk his own life to help a stranger.

Throughout the entire trip to Brisbane only one person, a young cowboy – judging from his Stetson hat and riding boots – asked any questions about my injuries.

'What happened to your mate?' he said to King with the candidness of youth.

'Car accident,' King replied curtly. He turned to look out of the window, pointedly ending any further conversation.

In silence I thanked King for his compassion and diplomacy, for trying to protect me from further embarrassment.

I didn't know where we were going. King hadn't told me anything, except to say, 'I'll take you to Ted's place. You'll be safe there.'

From Tent to Buckingham Palace

When we touched down at the Eagle Farm airport in Brisbane, we took a cab to a doctor's surgery in Red Hill. There I was given a penicillin injection in my arm and my injuries were dressed. It was only a short drive from there to where Peter and I were to stay.

As the taxi pulled up outside Ted's house, I saw a short, slightly built man standing at the gate. He was of indeterminate age and although his body was slim, the large sinews in his bare arms told of a lifetime of hard work.

King introduced us. 'Audrey, this is Ted Buckingham. He'll be taking care of you from now on.'

We all went into the house. Ted's face was wreathed in smiles and his grey eyes were lit with laughter as he tried at once to make me smile.

With a slight stutter, he said, 'Who, who, who won?'

There was a short silence as the joke hit the floor with a silent thud and I intercepted a warning glance from King.

Ted cleared his throat and said, 'Right, bad joke, sorry.' He really was sorry and, had I not been so distressed, I would have quipped back with the answer to this stale old joke: 'I did but you should've seen the other fellow.'

Ted cleared his throat again, 'Ahem,' and spat, sending a globule of spit out of the kitchen window, narrowly missing a giant marmalade-striped cat that sat sleeping on the windowsill.

I was totally exhausted. Timidly I asked Ted if he would show us where Peter and I were to sleep.

I didn't know it then, but Ted Buckingham with his stutter and warped sense of humour was to provide us with the stability and security that we needed if we were ever to recover at all.

∞

Time had no meaning for me again, just as at the campsite. There was no reason for us to go anywhere or to do anything. Ted saw that we had everything we needed. He went shopping and bought us food and clothing out of his own pocket. I was aware of Ted and Peter coming and going. I knew I was speaking to them but didn't remember anything that was said. Ted cooked and brought me meals and cups of tea in bed. He waited on me hand and foot. But, most importantly, he cared for Peter.

I don't know how long I lay in this dreamlike state, drifting in and out of consciousness, not quite knowing what was real and what a dream. But gradually I began to take notice of my surroundings. I saw that I was lying in an iron bed just like the one Mum used to have. It had large brass knobs on the bed-poles and white ceramic pieces painted with coloured flowers set into the black framework. The bed jingled when you got into or out of it or simply turned over. The room was large and sparsely furnished. Apart from the bed, the only other furniture was a solid silky-oak double wardrobe and a washstand with a jug and basin.

The ceiling was very high. I estimated that it was close to twelve or thirteen feet. There was a single, bare, flyspecked light globe hanging from the ceiling on the end of a black cord. It emitted a yellow, dull glow, as if its life was almost exhausted. The walls were made of narrow panels, each about three inches in width. There was one sash window in the room, covered by two heavy cretonne curtains.

As I lay in bed the sound of heavy vehicles and people's voices that came and went at intervals began to puzzle me. The voices sounded so close, yet muffled. At first I thought they were outside my bedroom door. Then I realised they were outside my window.

I got out of bed and drew the curtains aside and was instantly blinded by the bright daylight. A sharp pain shot across my forehead as I struggled to focus. But as my eyes gradually became accustomed to the brightness, I saw that the window looked out onto a wide verandah and then onto the street.

The house was low-set with a public footpath a little more than a metre from the front steps. Just then a City Council bus pulled up level with the front gate and people boarded the bus. That explained all the strange noises I had been hearing. It was an eerie feeling knowing that the bed where I had been sleeping was only two metres from where people were coming and going at all hours of the day and night.

Ted had been kind, but I could not impose on him any longer. I had no clothes to speak of and no money, so as soon as my wounds were healed I started to frequent hotel lounge bars. Despite all I had been through I was still good-looking enough to attract male attention. It wasn't long before men who were willing to pay for sex approached me. I would take them to a third-rate hotel that rented rooms by the hour.

∞

When Peter and I escaped from Arnold, we left with only the clothes we were wearing and Peter's little school port in which I had hidden photos and letters. All of our other family and personal treasures were left behind.

Throughout the whole journey from the Windorah campsite to Red Hill, Peter had hardly spoken. He responded in monosyllables when spoken to directly, but he was still emotionless and remote. I hadn't counted on the long-term psychological damage the abuse and spiritual deprivation had done to him and just thought that once we were safely out of my husband's reach, Peter, being a child, would bounce back and be his bright and happy self again. But Peter never did recover: he remained solitary and introverted, unable to show affection or emotion outwardly from then on. How bitterly I regretted allowing us to be placed in so much danger. It seemed to me that I had travelled to Windorah with one child and returned to Brisbane with another.

Peter had learning difficulties at school. His teacher complained that he just sat and stared out of the window all day. He didn't appear to hear her speaking to him. It was as if he had escaped into another world. I knew very well what she meant by this. I recalled my own school days when, as an unhappy schoolgirl, I had sat daydreaming of a place where there were no cruel people or cruel schools. I knew where Peter had run to and why he had run.

Peter Is Missing

Because Peter couldn't sleep at night I often took him to the local picture theatre at Red Hill. I didn't like the pictures so I would take him there and pick him up afterwards at about eleven o'clock. But one night I fell asleep, and when I awoke it was one o'clock in the morning. I jumped up and went into Peter's room hoping he'd be there, but his bed had not been slept in.

Frantically, I ran up the road searching the footpaths and the gutters in case he had been hit by a car or had fallen down and hit his head. All sorts of possibilities were running through my head, all of them bad.

When I reached the theatre it was deserted and in darkness.

For a moment I stood there, shaking badly. I sank to my knees, held my head in my hands, and sobbed. Then suddenly, for no reason, my fear disappeared and I became calm. It was as if someone had spoken to me, though I had heard no voice, and he told me he was locked inside the theatre.

I ran the few yards along Musgrave Road to the Red Hill Police Station in Waterworks Road. No one answered my frantic knocking so I ran back past the theatre to a nearby telephone booth and rang the Roma Street Police Station.

While I waited for the police, I prayed that Peter would be asleep and not realise he was locked in the theatre. It seemed to take an eternity.

When they finally arrived I ran to the road and, before they could get out of the car, I begged them to hurry. 'My son is locked inside the theatre,' I said, 'and if he wakes up he'll be terrified.' But they ignored me. Instead of opening the door with a skeleton key, one of them casually lit a cigarette while the other took out a notebook.

'Calm down, lady,' the one with the notebook said. 'What is your son's name?'

'Peter,' I said abruptly. I wanted to scream. 'He's in the theatre, in the dark.' I began to cry again, frustrated by their slowness and what appeared to be an uncaring attitude.

Suddenly, the other policeman flicked his cigarette into the gutter and came to life.

'What was he wearing when you last saw him?' he asked.

'What does it matter what he was wearing?' I responded angrily. 'He's in the theatre.'

'Lady, there's a million-to-one chance that your son is locked inside the theatre. The staff check the place before they close up. It's more likely he's been picked up on his way home. Now what was he wearing? It will help us to find him faster.'

'If you will just open the door, you will find him faster still,' I said sarcastically.

Finally, I was so persistent and so positive that they decided to ring the manager and ask him to come down and open the door. The manager arrived promptly in his pyjamas and dressing gown, and they found Peter, sound asleep, stretched out on one of the canvas seats in the front row of the theatre.

1953–1956

Strangers when we meet

In the years after my mother died, my father, sisters and brothers rarely saw each other. Except for my sister Helen, who lived with her husband, Bob, and her children, the rest of us weren't permanently settled. That is, we had no permanent place to call our own. It seemed that when my mother died so did the stability of our home. Even Dad was drifting; his home was wherever he managed to hang his hat. It was as if my mother was the anchor holding our family together, and when she was gone we were cast adrift.

Sometimes members of the family would meet by accident. One would ask, 'How are you going?' The other would reply, 'I'm okay. Have you seen any of the others around?' 'No.' 'Okay, see you around.' Then, with a wave of the hand, they would disappear into the crowd. There were times when I wanted to run after them, to ask, 'Can I come with you? Will you look after me even for a little while?' But I never did. They were no better equipped to survive than I was.

Then one day, purely by chance, I met my father.

I was standing on the corner of Queen and Edward streets, waiting for the traffic lights to change, when for some inexplicable reason I glanced behind me at the tall gentleman standing there. At first he didn't see me; he was looking straight ahead.

As always he was immaculately dressed. It was a warm day so he wasn't wearing his coat, just his dark blue suit-pants, a white shirt with chrome stretch armbands and a dark blue tie. And as always he wore his grey fedora squarely upon his head.

I was still looking at him when the lights changed and people surged forward. But I didn't move, and he almost walked over the top of me.

'Freddie?' my father asked, incredulously.

'Yes,' I replied, laughing.

'Well, I'll be damned, fancy running into you like this.'

As the crowd was gathering at the lights again, we moved back onto the footpath out of the crush of people. I was happy to see him, because in spite of all that had happened I still loved my father.

'How have you been getting on, Freddie?' Dad asked.

'Fine,' I said. But I would have said that regardless of how I felt. My world was too disruptive to expect anyone to understand, even my father. 'Have you seen any of the girls?'

'I haven't seen Jan or Esmae for a long time,' he said, shaking his head, 'but Mary is staying with Patrick up on Harvey Range, about thirty miles out of Townsville.'

I told him that Peter and I were staying at Red Hill with

a fellow named Ted Buckingham and he suggested that he come back with me. So we caught the bus home to Ted's place and that night Dad slept on the lounge. The next day he fixed himself up a bed on the verandah and just moved in. He was drinking heavily, but Dad and Ted got on very well together and Ted didn't seem to mind him being there.

1957, Aged 23

My brother Rod

One day my brother Rod came to our house when no one was home. He was a bit drunk and said, 'Dad tells me you are working the hotels selling sex.' I was ashamed and didn't answer.

'Well,' he said, 'I don't blame you, all women are whores; some get paid, some do it for fun. It all adds up to the same thing – they use men for their own ends then throw them over.'

What happened next remains in my mind as some sort of nightmare.

Rod grabbed me from behind, put his hand on my breasts and, with his other hand, began groping under my dress.

I struggled free. 'For Christ's sake, Rod, what do you think you're doing? I'm your sister.'

He became very angry. 'You're just a common moll. I'm no different to any other bloke you have sex with except I'm not going to pay you.' Then Rod struck me across the face with the back of his hand with such force I was thrown to the floor. He grabbed me and dragged me into the bedroom.

As I pleaded with him to stop he punched me several times again in the face. I knew I couldn't stop him now. In his eyes I could see the lust as I had seen it many times before from this same position. He pinned me down on the bed. Then he raped me.

Afterwards he left without saying a word or even looking at me. He could not or would not meet my eyes.

Neither I nor any of my family ever saw my brother Rod again.

∞

When my father came home he asked, 'What happened to you?'

I couldn't tell him what my brother had done – or of the utter degradation I felt. I didn't want to ever speak of it again.

But I had to explain the swelling and bruising of my face and throat.

I made up a story of a man who had refused to pay me. He had assaulted me before he left the hotel. I realised later that I had basically described what my brother had done – I just concealed his identity. I thought my father might blame me. I had always known his attitude towards women being raped. He said they must have led the bloke on and they got what they deserved.

But I should have known what would come next. My father said, 'The bastard. Well, that won't happen again. Bring them home here.'

So I did. My father was waiting at the front door and took the money before the men were allowed in.

I felt a part of me die inside.

∞

During this period my father mentioned several times how he wished he had a block of land to settle down on. He talked about putting up a shed to live in while he built his own house.

'I would live there happily until I died,' he said.

So I bought my father a piece of land in Kingston with money saved from working as a prostitute. But he never lived there and when I asked why, he said, 'It's too lonely, Fred. I don't want to be on my own. I want to live with you.'

I felt great pity for him then. I was aware that he was sick, and I don't know what eventually happened to the land. I didn't want to know, either. I just knew what it had cost me in human suffering.

September 1957

The bridge

I was twenty-three years old when I decided to take my own life. I remember it was a bitterly cold night and I was wearing a heavy coat. I had been drunk for several days and, although I was sober then, I was very hungover. I was also very depressed. Before going to the bridge, I had been wandering the streets for hours. Ted and Dad were away working and, as so often, I didn't have anywhere to sleep and I had no money.

My family and friends had long since given me up as a lost cause because I wouldn't stop boozing. They would say things like 'pull yourself together' and 'why don't you get a job?', or 'act your age' and 'settle down', or 'get up and help yourself'. All of these suggestions were very fine but nobody could tell me how to cope with the severe depression I experienced when I wasn't drunk. I felt so alone and unwanted. I just wanted to die.

I was a failure as a mother. I had failed my sons Peter and tiny baby Ben, and I was a failure as a person because I couldn't even take care of myself.

When I went to the Victoria Bridge late that night, it was deserted. I stood there looking down into the murky depths and thinking that it couldn't be any harder to die than it was to live. Still, I was a terrible coward and I think I chose the bridge as a way out because once I jumped I couldn't change my mind. It didn't occur to me then that this attempt on my life could be another failure to add to a long list.

I climbed over the iron railing and sat on a steel outcrop about forty feet above the river.

But I had waited too long. Suddenly there were people standing at the railing where before there had been no one. Someone was talking to me although I couldn't hear what they were saying because of the loud roaring in my ears. A dark figure was climbing over the rail.

I felt them grab my hand.

For a moment, I thought of climbing back over the rail because I didn't really want to die. But, I thought, what do I have to go back to? Only imprisonment in the mental hospital for the rest of my life.

No, I couldn't face that.

I pulled free. At last my mind was made up. I jumped.

The fall from the bridge was one of the most enjoyable sensations I have ever experienced. I had expected to fall at a terrifying speed and to hit the water and die on impact. Instead, I drifted in slow motion, seeming to float gently down for ages. I felt somehow that someone was looking after me and I was not afraid. I remember thinking that I must have already hit the water and I was dead.

The myth of becoming an angel and flying up to heaven when you died now seemed a reality. But no sooner had this thought crossed my mind than the world exploded in a flash of bright light – and my face was in the mud at the bottom of the river.

I was suffocating, but then I started to drift to the surface. I looked up and I could see the light on top of the water. It still seemed like an eternity before I finally reached the surface and I was able to breathe again.

I was so tired I just lay floating on top of the water, not caring what happened to me. I wanted to go to sleep there in the water. I think I was close to drowning.

∞

Suddenly, again there were people, pulling at me, dragging me into a small boat. I heard someone say, 'She is unconscious.' I wanted to tell them that I wasn't unconscious, I was just too tired to open my eyes; but I couldn't think of the words, so I simply lay there and went to sleep.

Somewhere far away I could hear men's voices and again they were pulling at me – would they never let me alone? I felt myself being lifted under the arms by a very strong man who was lifting me up high into the air and I thought for a moment he was trying to lift me back up onto the bridge. 'Silly man,' I thought, 'he couldn't reach up that high.' Someone grasped my hands and tried to pull me up. Then the boat capsized and we all fell back into the water.

Suddenly, I was no longer tired, I was fighting for my life. My head was being repeatedly bashed against a metal surface, as I was dragged under the boat on a fast outgoing tide.

My lungs were at bursting point when I broke to the surface once more. Looming high above me was a moored barge, but the people were nowhere in sight. I couldn't see the bridge any more either and this meant I had been swept around a bend in the river and was being washed out to sea. I was terribly frightened and exhausted.

I had had enough of this dying business; all I wanted now was to get out of the water. I saw some jetty pylons ahead of me, so I reached out to grab one as the force of the tide rushed me past. As I moved from pylon to pylon, I realised my hands were cut and bleeding from the barnacles. For the first time since I had plunged into the water I recalled my father's repeated warnings: 'Never swim in the Brisbane River, because it's full of sharks.' I was bordering now on hysteria and it took a great deal of effort for me to regain control. I knew I must first find a way to get out of the water. Nothing else mattered.

Finally, I came to some stone steps that reached almost to the water. They were wet and slippery with slime but I managed to drag myself up on my hands and knees. The smell of those steps, a mixture of fish, salt water and dank decay, still fills me with dread.

After what seemed like a very long time, I reached the top of the stairs and collapsed on the wooden wharf. A man's rough yet kindly voice awakened me, saying, 'Come on, mate, the water police are searching for you.' He wrapped me in a blanket and carried me inside a building.

Part Four

Of Unsound Mind

It was several days before I was actually *aware* again. But, when I was fully conscious, I saw that I was in a small cell, about six-feet square. The long, loose gown I was wearing was not mine, and I was lying on a foul-smelling mattress on a floor that reeked of stale urine. There was nothing else in the room. There was no window, just a long narrow glass panel no more than six inches wide set in the centre of the door.

A long time passed before anyone came to see me. Several times I went and looked through the glass panel, but all I could see was a long, deserted, dimly lit corridor. I tried to open the door but there was no handle. I felt a rising hysteria within me – I was a prisoner and I didn't know where I was.

Terrified, I huddled in a corner with my knees drawn up under my chin and my arms wrapped tightly around my legs. I felt so alone, so small and vulnerable, I wished that I could die. I asked God to help me. But He didn't answer.

Maybe Dad was right, maybe there wasn't any God. I tried to pray but I didn't know how; all I could remember was 'Our Father who lives in Heaven'.

Imprisoned in this cell, I tried hard to hang on to the last bit of sanity I had left. Finally the tears spilled over and I cried and sobbed so hard my stomach hurt and I wet myself.

∞

Several days later when nobody came to claim me, I was transferred to the Goodna Mental Hospital and committed as being *of unsound mind*. Labels such as suicidal, schizophrenic, psychoneurosis and psychopathic personality were attached to me. Again I was given electroconvulsive therapy – also known by then as shock treatment – along with a frightening array of drugs.

Peg Connor

I suppose reaching out to Peg Connor at this time showed the level of my desperation. But that is what I did. There was nobody left who would take me out of the hospital. So, a year older, on 28 September 1958 I made a deal with her. I promised to come back to Drake Street if she would have me released into her care. How ironic it was. The Mental Health Board released me into the care of a brothel keeper and numerous other unsuitable carers because I couldn't look after myself.

I would not remain at the house for long. The Health Department did not pursue escapees or defaulters, and I just needed enough money to buy some clothes and a train ticket. Somewhere along the way I had lost almost everything I owned, except the white dress that was still at the house. So I planned carefully to stay only four weeks with Peg, then find work on a station property and never return to the city, ever!

1958–1960

I got a job on Thorny Downs station as a housemaid and laundress. It was a very good place to work. Mrs Jenkins, my boss, was a pleasant woman who expected you to do your job without supervision. This kind of trust brought out the best in people, including me. Mrs Jenkins, or Bonnie as she liked to be called, reminded me a lot of Mrs Kemp. She was a large-boned, strong woman, but, unlike Mrs Kemp, Bonnie had a placid disposition and a pleasant face that lit up when she smiled.

I stayed on at Thorny Downs for two years. During that time, I had long conversations with Bonnie, and confided to her that I was legally still a patient of the mental hospital. Bonnie rang a solicitor for legal advice on my behalf. The solicitor told her, 'A patient need only prove they have a permanent place to live and the means to support themselves.'

So I returned to Goodna Mental Hospital and, for the last time, secured my own release. I was a free woman again.

My stay in the country had filled me with renewed hope and I began to rebuild my life. I was not, however, under any illusions that my mental state, though it was stable at this time, would not shatter if placed under strain.

Nevertheless, I went to Sydney and brought Peter back to Brisbane. I planned to take him back to Thorny Downs station with me.

Then I met David.

August 1960, Aged 26

A chance encounter

I first met David in the Grand Central Hotel in Queen Street, Brisbane. I was sitting alone waiting for a friend, whom I knew only as Blisters due to the ever-present Band-Aids on her toes and heels. Blisters and I had arranged to meet at seven o'clock that night, to have a drink and go to the pictures. It was now seven-thirty and I decided to leave and go to the pictures alone. Just then, a noisy bunch of young soldiers entered the bar.

As I stood up, one young man detached himself from the group and approached my table.

I didn't look at him, but picked up my handbag and retrieved my jacket from the back of the chair. So I was taken aback when this young man took my jacket from me. The impulse to snatch it back was strong, but I allowed him to hold it while I slipped it on. He was very good-looking, with an open face and a ready smile, a man of medium height with black hair and blue eyes.

'I'm David,' he said politely.

'I'm Audrey,' I replied, and we very formally shook hands.

'Will you have dinner with me?' he asked with an engaging smile.

My first response was to refuse. Yet he seemed different somehow from other men I had met, and I wanted to find out more about him. I accepted.

'Where would you like to go?' I asked courteously.

'Your choice.' He laughed. 'I'm new in town.'

'Okay,' I said, 'I know just the place.'

The Shingle Inn was small and quaint, with dim lights and an old-world English theme. After dinner, David hailed a taxi, stopped to pick up some beer and we went back home to Ted's place, which I was living in again.

David and I talked and drank into the small hours of the morning. When he fell asleep on the settee I covered him with a blanket and went to bed myself.

In the morning, as I drove him back to the army camp at Enoggera, David asked if he could see me again.

'Yes,' I replied, trying not to sound too eager.

'Only thing is I'm going away up north on a training exercise.'

'When?'

David looked down at his hands, and after a short pause said, 'Tomorrow.'

'Oh, so soon! How long will you be gone?'

This time he didn't hesitate. 'Six weeks.'

I kissed him lightly on the lips and said, 'See you in six weeks.'

Over the next few months our friendship deepened into a trusting and meaningful relationship. Gradually I confided to David my life story. I told him about the house in Drake Street, my health problems, marriage to Arnold and the dramatic rescue by King Cole. Rather than deter him, my story made David even more protective of Peter and me.

King Cole

A week before my twenty-sixth birthday, King Cole came in from the bush and gave me a birthday present, a bottle of Black Narcissus perfume. I was pleasantly surprised by his gift, because I had seen King only twice since we had left the campsite, each time for a brief visit. 'Just to see you're getting on all right, mate,' King explained.

That night over a few drinks David and King got to know each other. It was a good evening, without any hint of drama. Still, I was puzzled when, before he left, King turned an empty glass upside down and said, 'Let's drink to the departed.'

Around one o'clock, King drove David back to the barracks. I didn't hear anything more that night.

The following morning Ted found King dead in his car outside the house. He had driven back and shot himself through the head. Peter had been woken by the noise, but thought it was a car backfiring.

I was devastated by this death. Later I thought how ironic it was that King had given me back my life, only to take his own.

The Good Years

In December 1960, David asked me to marry him. Up until then all attempts to serve Arnold with a divorce writ had failed. To prevent Arnold from ever worrying Peter and me again, I had told Helen I was going to charge Arnold with assault. But he disappeared. Another irony. Now I couldn't find him. It was to be twenty years before we were finally divorced.

Nevertheless, two weeks before Christmas, David, Peter and I moved into a flat together in Kelvin Grove, just ten minutes north of the city by tram. This proved to be a significant turning point in my life.

Peter was ten years old now. In the years that followed he and David grew to love each other. It was a love that was to last a lifetime. They did all the 'man things' together: sailing little boats on the pond in the Botanical Gardens, fishing at Dohle's Rocks, and flying toy aeroplanes in open fields. They were good mates.

Over the next twenty-seven years, David worked to make me happy. He was a kind and gentle man and, although I was often difficult to get along with, he never blamed me for anything. His love was stronger than I could ever return.

He responded to my crying and unexplained fear, feelings of helplessness and angry outbursts, with calmness and forgiveness. 'Stop beating up on yourself,' he would say kindly, 'it's not your fault.' This was the first time anyone had shown any understanding. The medical profession, my family and friends had failed to recognise the extent and helplessness of my suffering and distress. It took someone who loved me to understand, and this above all allowed the healing process to begin.

1961, aged 27 years

After a year, David, Peter and I moved to a house in Zillmere. It was a new house and I loved it. But David was still in the army and had to go away on six-week training exercises on a regular basis. This was the hardest part, because when David wasn't home at night I became very frightened. It was a fear I couldn't explain. I went to my local doctor and asked him to prescribe something to help me sleep at night, but when I couldn't explain what it was I was frightened of, he refused. I went to many doctors after this; I cried and begged for help until they threw me out of the office. One doctor threatened to have me locked up in the lunatic asylum if I ever came back.

So for years I lived like this, going into deep depression as evening approached. I imagined I had a brain tumour that turned me into a Jekyll and Hyde character.

At this time I began to experience severe migraine headaches. One day while David was away on training exercises, the headaches became so bad I lay in a darkened room for two days. On the third day, with no relief in sight, I struggled out of bed, and with a red haze in front of my eyes, I went to the tram stop and caught a tram to the doctor's surgery at the top of the hill.

As I entered the waiting room, I saw it was full of patients. The very thought of waiting for an hour or more, in so much pain, made me feel sick, and suddenly I wanted to throw up. I staggered from the surgery and barely made it to the gutter before I vomited. By the time I was finished I was gasping for breath and crying.

I felt someone touch me on the shoulder. It was a man in a white coat. I saw his face through a red haze, aware only that he was speaking to me.

'I'm a pharmacist,' he said. 'My shop is just here next to the doctor's surgery.' I translated this into a chemist shop. 'Did you want to see the doctor?' he asked kindly.

'There's too many people, and I can't sit there. I've had a migraine for three days,' I said sobbing.

'Come with me,' he said, firmly gripping my elbow. I went without protest. It didn't matter if he was leading me to the guillotine, I went like a lamb. I would do anything to stop the pain.

The chemist led me to a chair. 'Wait here,' he said. 'I'll only be a minute.' He returned almost immediately with a medicine glass of liquid. 'Drink this,' he said. 'It will stop the pain.'

I didn't ask what it was and he didn't tell me. I simply drank the liquid in one swallow, its wet coolness soothing my dry throat.

The chemist placed a cold compress on my forehead. 'You rest for a while,' he said. 'You'll soon be feeling better.'

In a few minutes I felt the hammering inside my head begin to ease. The pain, like a living thing that attacked me from within my head, began to slink away to the deepest recesses of my brain. Soon, I don't know how long, I opened my eyes and I could see clearly again. The red haze had disappeared and the pain had become just a dull ache.

'Thank you, I feel much better,' I said to the chemist, 'but I'm sorry, I don't have any money to pay you.'

'That's okay,' he said with a wave of his hand, 'I'm just happy I was able to help.'

∞

Each night, just as twilight set in, I would load my rifle and sit up all night absolutely certain someone was trying to break in. I would imagine I saw the window curtains begin to open. I stared at them so intently my eyes and neck ached, and eventually I thought I saw them draw back and a white drowned face appear. Then, as the sun came up, I would drop into an exhausted sleep. But I realise now that the curtains didn't really move and there wasn't anyone out there, either. Neither was I a dual personality. These were all symptoms of major depression. It was all a part of living in a depressed state without medication. Brandy was the only medication I had to relieve my fear.

But brandy was expensive as well. David and I still weren't married and he was trying to keep me and my child on a single man's army pay – about seventeen pounds a week, as the army did not recognise a *de facto* relationship. We were very poor for a long time but we were happy together, and although Peter could never bring himself to call David 'Dad', he loved him with all his heart.

Gradually, with David's help, I learned to control my emotions. He said, 'When you feel like hitting someone or yelling your head off, just pretend you are somewhere else. Switch off and think about something nice. That's what I used to do in the orphanage,' he added. 'I thought about my dog "Rags" that I had back in England.' That was when I found out how difficult David's life had been.

David was born in Leicestershire, England, in 1935. His mother was an invalid and his father worked in a stocking factory. There were four boys and two girls in the family. David was the eldest. During World War II, David and his brothers would watch the 'fireworks', as they called it. They were, in fact, watching the bombing of the city of Coventry by German planes. When David was ten years old his mother died. Soon after, his father brought them to Australia and immediately placed them all in an orphanage in Perth, Western Australia. The four children remained there until they turned eighteen and were allowed to leave. Their father never came back for them. At eighteen David joined the army.

So, the person who was to nurse me back to health was someone who had known great suffering too. There is a saying, *No one can take you down a path that they have not travelled before.*

It took me several years to master self-control. It wasn't as simple as just 'switching off', as David called it. Nevertheless, David knew what he was trying to say; he just didn't know how to explain it. Diverting my anger from one source to another until the crisis passed allowed me to control my emotions. Over time, I became a more socially acceptable person. This in turn developed my feelings of self-worth and self-esteem. Timidly at first, I began to come back into the real world.

In 1963, David and I were invited to a Christmas party at the army barracks. In the first few years of our marriage, I had declined to go out or mix with his friends. Not that I didn't want to, but I was afraid of people and particularly crowds. So when David asked, 'How about it, you feeling up to a party?' I surprised myself by saying, 'I'll give it a try, it might be fun.'

The only party dress I owned was the white dress with the pastel pink flowers. How I wished it had puffed sleeves, I felt so exposed with my bare armpits. I shortened the long skirt to waltz length, fastened the front with clips, and wore a white rope petticoat underneath. David said it looked smashing.

It was a wonderful night. The huge Christmas tree was lit with fairy lights, the band was playing, people were dancing, and it was such a party as I had never experienced before. Magical. David and I joined other couples in laughing and singing all night.

After this, I continued to improve and, although I still had occasional relapses, they were never serious enough to get me into trouble. Nevertheless, David made sure that I was never returned to the mental hospital, ever.

June 1968, Aged 34

Caring for Dad

We moved to Kallangur, an outer northern suburb of Brisbane. My dad was living in a flat in Newmarket, quite close to the city. One day when I was visiting him, Dad admitted that he had not felt well for some time, and he would like to go to the hospital for a checkup. This was out of character for my father because he disliked hospitals and did not trust doctors. So the very next day I took him to the Royal Brisbane Hospital.

After several tests, he was admitted to hospital and diagnosed as suffering from the kidney disease nephritis.

I asked the doctor what caused this disease. I felt sure the methylated spirits Dad had taken to habitually drinking had finally eaten his kidneys away.

'No, no,' the doctor replied emphatically. 'The spirits are not to blame, it is the Bex powders that have caused the damage.'

Bex Powders and their counterpart, Vincent's Powders, were both known as APC powders, because they contained three highly potent drugs: aspirin, phenacetin and caffeine. They were freely available from corner stores, supermarkets, newsagents and garages, in fact anywhere at all. They were sold to young children as well as adults, and there was no restriction on quantity. When used in moderation they were a powerful analgesic as well as a general pick-me-up. For this reason it was not unusual for bored housewives sharing a gossip to hand around the Vincent's/Bex and a glass of water in place of the more conventional coffee and biscuit. Perhaps habitual dieting had something to do with that, too. But once hooked on APCs, you stayed hooked, and there was an unlimited supply at the ridiculously low price of one penny per powder. No doubt there was an unprecedented number of deaths in the Aboriginal communities, too, that were only ever reported as kidney failure. Had all the deaths from kidney failure been truthfully recorded as APC poisoning, the drug companies would have been forced to withdraw those products from sale sooner.

But there was a cover-up, especially when the drug companies became aware that the eventual outcome of APC toxicity was irreversible damage to the kidneys. This is what the doctor said had happened to my father. He asked me if I knew how many powders my father had taken a day, but I couldn't tell him, because Dad was so secretive about them. When the doctor told me that my father had admitted to taking twelve I was shocked. More so when he added, 'It was probably more.'

When Dad was staying with me, he had Bex hidden all over the house; there were so many hiding places, I couldn't help running into them. But I knew he only took them when he wasn't drinking, and I had wrongly figured they were the lesser of two evils.

Soon after this these drugs were removed from the shelves of shops and became prescription drugs only. A little too late for my father, and no doubt countless other mothers and fathers.

My father comes home

Several times I was called to the hospital when my father was not expected to last the night. I sat with him through the dark hours but each time he rallied by morning and we began to hope again.

One night I entered the ward and saw a Roman Catholic priest giving Dad the last rites. Apparently, my father had been baptised in the Catholic religion, and the priest was called when they thought once more that he was dying.

At that moment Dad woke up and pushed the priest away, saying, 'Get out of here, what do you think you're doing? Go on, take your rot somewhere else!'

Then one day the doctor told me I could take my father home. I thought this was good news. Only later was I to learn that Dad's illness was terminal: they had sent him home from the hospital to die. In fact, they had decided to withhold further treatment with the dialysis machine and let him die of natural causes.

Outside the weather was grey and overcast and as I sat and looked through the window, I saw my sister Helen, who lived only five houses away, standing at her front door. I wondered if she would come to see her father now. She was still angry because Dad had chosen to live with me instead of her.

It was around seven o'clock in the morning and I knew my dad was nearing the end of his suffering, and I was happy for him. The doctor had felt sure he would not live through the night. If I had had the means to painlessly release him before this, I would have done so. The law does not allow an animal to suffer needlessly, yet they will not accord a human being the same consideration.

David had been in two minds about whether he should go to work that morning, but he had taken so much time off since Dad had come home, he had to take the chance Dad would last a little longer.

That morning I prepared my father a small bowl of baby-food custard, even though I knew he would not eat it. He hadn't taken any nourishment for several days. Even so, I still had to make this token offer, because I felt so inadequate and I didn't know what else to do.

So my feelings were mixed when I went back into the bedroom and saw my father sitting on the edge of the bed, swinging his legs back and forth (his feet could touch the floor when I first brought him home from hospital). I couldn't believe it. A few moments before he had been too weak to raise his hand to signal that he wanted me. Now he was sitting up looking at his fingernails.

When he saw me in the doorway he said, 'Look at my nails, the pink is coming back.' But I wasn't looking at his nails, I was looking at his face. It was still the same ashen colour as it had been all the night before.

What was I to think? I knew I should have been happy to see such a transformation, but I wasn't. I thought there was something terribly wrong and I was afraid. I had walked into the room expecting to see my father either dead or near death, only to be confronted with a smiling caricature of a dead man.

The smile did not reach his eyes; they were still a dull, vacant grey. I tried not to show how frightened I was, how my body was being besieged with wave after wave of tingling electricity, leaving me breathless and weak.

Then, abruptly, this was over – my father slumped forward, and would have fallen to the floor had I not jumped forward to catch him.

That was something I could deal with. I settled him gently back on the bed, and went to work straightening the bedclothes and generally trying to make him comfortable. But suddenly I heard a strange gurgling sound coming from his throat.

Thinking he was having difficulty breathing, I turned him on his side. It didn't help. The gurgling continued.

I rang the doctor and told him of the strange sight I had just witnessed, as well as the noise my father was making. The doctor assured me there was nothing to be frightened of. 'Dying people sometimes display a last burst of energy just before the end,' he said. 'A sort of final discharge of the body's battery before the spark is extinguished.' The noise, the doctor explained, is commonly known as the death rattle – also a symptom that Dad's end was near.

∞

The doctor promised he would come straight away, but he didn't. It would be hours before he arrived.

In the meantime, I desperately needed to be with somebody. I was physically and emotionally drained and I wasn't sure I could cope much longer, I felt I was going out of my mind. I had telephoned David at the Enoggera Army Barracks and left a message for him to return home immediately.

I was desperate, so I walked down the road and called to my sister from the front gate. 'Dad is close to the end, Helen . . . will you come and see him now?'

'I can't,' she said. 'I have to cut the kids' lunches for school, I'll come later.'

Neither Dad nor I needed her later, we needed her now. I turned and, with tears streaming down my face, I ran quickly back to the house.

Except for my father, I was alone in the house. I looked at him lying in the old-fashioned iron double bed he always liked so much. I saw his decrepit and pathetically thin body that hardly raised a mound beneath the pale blue coverlet. Where his head rested on the flat pillow it made a small hollow.

Over the past few weeks I had seen the pain etch new lines in his dear face. The crinkles around his eyes and nose, which once had heralded laughter, now were hardened into permanent furrows of pain. I looked into my father's eyes, and saw that, where once there had been a fiery blue colour, the fire had now gone out, leaving only cold grey ashes within. I recalled my mother's words when, as a hurt and troubled little girl, I had stared into the fire: 'If you pour your worries into the fire, they will return to you as ashes, and trouble you no more.'

Now, as I saw the ashes in my father's eyes, I knew his troubles were over. The tears, grief and sorrow I felt now were for myself, and for my loss, not for my father. He was soon in a deep coma, his breathing coming only at intervals.

Not long after – I don't know how long – while I stroked his hair and held his hand, my dad journeyed to that place from which no traveller returns. And if any dreams did come after death, I hoped, for my father's sake, they were not of this world. I hoped he had left his hell behind him.

Death of a King

It was just a little before eight in the morning, and as I pulled the sheet up over his face, my tears spilled over and I cried for the loss of a man I once thought was a king. Somehow it was incredibly hard to believe that this skeletal scrap of humanity was once a Goliath who had defied swollen rivers by carrying me across them and defied doctors by picking me up in his arms and carrying me out of the psychiatric ward. Was this the same man who had once looked the whole world in the eye and defied it to answer back? How very like Ozymandias we are. How very vulnerable and expendable we all are in the end.

While I was still in the room, I heard David calling to me, and I ran to meet him. We fell into each other's arms and together we wept and tenderly comforted each other. As I softly whispered to David that he was too late to say goodbye, he answered, 'It doesn't matter, I already told him that I loved him, and that's better than saying goodbye.'

Hours later the doctor arrived, and pronounced my father dead.

As the doctor turned towards the front door to leave, David said, 'What will I do with the body?' Until then I had not given a thought to how we were to dispose of it. We had never had a dead person in the house before.

As David said afterwards, he thought the doctor would take Dad away, and he was quite prepared to help the doctor carry Dad's body out to his car and lay him on the back seat.

For a moment a painful look came over the doctor's face. I could see he had visions of David burying my father down the backyard. Obviously, he had not been asked that question before either, yet it was the most logical thing in the world for a person to ask, especially if they had never had to deal with this sort of thing before.

For a moment or two the doctor was at a loss for words. 'Well, er, nothing, er, *don't touch it!*' he finally got out. Then he asked, 'Which funeral home have you engaged? I will advise them to come and transport the body to their premises.'

I suppose it did seem silly but neither David nor I had thought about the funeral. I don't think we really thought my father would die, not just yet anyway; he had been on the verge of death for so long, I think we just got used to the idea.

'We haven't made any arrangements,' David replied. 'How were we supposed to know just when he would die? Besides, it sounds a bit cold-blooded to be making arrangements to bury a man before he is even dead.' I could see the logic in that.

So when we finally did make these arrangements and the men from the funeral parlour arrived to take my father's body away, it was after midday, and I was lying down, so I didn't see them arrive.

When I heard someone bumping into doors and walls, though, and generally making a hell of a racket, I came out to find out what all the noise was about – just in time to see the undertaker walking ahead of me down the hallway.

I almost screamed at what they had done with my father's body. The container they had brought to transport Dad in looked like an oversized guitar case. It was made of tin and covered with leather. It had large leather straps and buckles, and two leather handles on the side, one at each end. The whole thing looked too small for my father to fit into.

I was extremely distressed to see Dad reduced to nothing but a port full of broken bones. How else could he have fitted into that bag? I thought.

In my hysteria and grief I asked them to open the port so I could see what they had done to him. David's strangled cry – '*No*' – and the way he looked, like he was going to faint, made me realise not only what I was asking, but what I was going to see if they complied.

So instead, I told them their method was callous, an unacceptable, indecent way to care for the dead.

∞

At his own request, my father was cremated at the Aspley Crematorium, following a simple service. Although my brother Patrick paid for the funeral, my sister Helen and I were the only members of our family who attended. I didn't want my father's ashes, so I left them at the crematorium. Not one of Dad's children ever inquired about their whereabouts, and I never told them.

Aged 35

Heading north to Giru

In 1968, after twelve years, David left the army. It had been a hard battle for us to survive on a single man's pay, but as a de facto couple that was all we were entitled to. There was little work in Brisbane so, when we read in the paper that the sugar season was about to start in Giru, I contacted my brother Patrick, who had lived and worked in Giru for many years. He helped us find a job and accommodation.

David, Peter and I packed the car and trailer with our belongings, our cat Tom and the pet galah, and headed north on the Bruce Highway. It was a long, gruelling trek to Giru, and our little old Austin car limped along, making a valiant effort to tow the fully laden trailer. It was hot and dusty so we camped often along the way. Peter collected firewood and built a small fire to boil the billy, while David prepared canned meat sandwiches.

The trip was uneventful and, in two days, we arrived. The only accommodation available was an abandoned cane-cutters' barracks. It really was a terrible place, right on the edge of the canefields. But David and Peter, who was by now eighteen, each got a job in the sugar-mill.

The whole process of extracting the sugar from the cane was powered by steam. The waste sugar cane, called bagasse, provided fuel for the furnaces, which produced this steam. David and Peter worked alternately, either as Boiler Attendant or Fireman. The money was good and for a while we were able to save a little.

While David and Peter worked in the sugar-mill I worked in the fields stripping cane. Women were mostly employed for this job. Unlike the cane to be processed, which was cut by machine, this cane was cut by hand. Green and unburned, it was used for planting new crops.

We usually started in the early morning to get through a large volume of work before the heat and burning sun slowed us down. We wore long-sleeved shirts and trousers, as well as gloves, to protect us from the sun and biting insects. At this time of the morning – before sunup – mosquitoes that rose from the cane in a black cloud savagely attacked us.

The long cane stalks were piled high on the edge of a newly ploughed field. We had to strip all the leaves from the stalks and pack the neatly trimmed sugar cane on the ground, where at the end of the day they could be counted.

The cane toads

One of the great drawbacks of living so close to the canefields was the cane toad. It took a lot of courage for me to walk past or step over them when I needed to use the outdoor lavatory some fifteen yards from the house. The toads were so big even our cat was afraid of them. I was glad of that, because cane toads have a sac on their head containing a poisonous fluid that they excrete when attacked. If the poison is absorbed in the mouth, the victim is paralysed and death usually follows within a short time.

∞

Our lavatory, or 'dunny' as it was colloquially called, was a small outhouse made from corrugated iron, with a flat, slanted roof. Inside there was a wooden box seat over a black pan or drum lined with pitch.

Originally, the box seat was placed over a very deep hole in the ground. When the hole filled, it was covered with soil, and the whole building was moved to another site. However, by 1970 we were more civilised. New technology had replaced the open pit with the pan system and provided a weekly cleansing service. Our toilet paper of small squares of newspaper secured by a nail on the wall was also upgraded to the now familiar white toilet roll.

At the rear of the dunny, there was a trapdoor fastened on the outside with a large bolt. It was while I was seated there, early one morning when it was just breaking day, that I heard a terrific bang at the back of the dunny. At first, I thought the building was coming down on top of me. It all happened so fast I didn't even have time to get up before I was hit by a blast of cold air that froze my bum. The pan was dragged out from under me and another was shoved in its place.

I knew the night-carter man came and collected the pans once a week – but this was the first time that the pans had been changed while I was sitting on them!

The cane fires

Before the cane was harvested, it was burnt. At the first torching, hundreds of birds seemed to appear from nowhere. Flying just ahead of the flames, they feasted on all sorts of insects and vermin running ahead of the fire. Burning was always done at dusk, when the wind was low. It was a spectacular sight as field after field was lit and the flames leapt high in the air, lighting up the darkening sky.

Cane had not always been burnt before harvesting. In the early days it was cut green by the cane-cutters, who often died through contracting leptospirosis, or Weil's disease. This disease causes extremely high body temperatures that are difficult to control, and can result in death or brain damage.

Ironically, this was the same disease David had suffered from when he was stationed in Malaya. When David was discharged, his paybook was stamped 'retarded'.

Farmers were unaware for quite a long time that Weil's disease was caused by workers being exposed to the urine of feral animals such as rats. It was not until the early 1930s that they learned that burning the cane before harvesting could eliminate the disease. Still, the farmers were reluctant to do this because burning lowered the sugar content and this meant less profit.

1970, Aged 36

Travelling to Mount Isa

When the sugar-cane season ended, we had to move on. David heard Mount Isa Mines were employing men, so we decided to travel the six hundred miles inland to there.

As we travelled west along the Flinders Highway, we noticed how friendly everyone was. People were waving and shouting to us. We couldn't hear what they were saying, but we all waved back to them anyway. That is, until a car came alongside and the driver yelled, 'Your trailer is on fire.' David slammed the brakes on so hard, the car skidded on the powdery bull-dust, and we were momentarily enveloped in a blinding cloud of dust. We all piled out of the car and saw smoke billowing out from under the canvas. One of us had carelessly thrown a cigarette butt from the car and it had landed on the canvas covering our load and burnt through to the mattress. Only the mattress was on fire, so David and

Peter dragged it off the trailer and beat out the flames. The mattress was ruined and we left it there on the roadside. Our galah was shrieking loudly, but was otherwise unharmed. We made the remainder of the trip without incident.

Anna James

Mount Isa is a lead and copper mining town in the far north west of Queensland. Peter, now twenty-one, was working underground, while David worked in the copper smelter.

It was February 1972 and we had been in Mount Isa for two years, when I received a phone call from a woman I had never met before named Anna. She was a friend of my sister Esmae and asked if she might call on David and me that evening because she had a proposition for us.

When David came home from work I told him of the strange telephone call.

'Well,' he said, in a matter-of-fact way, 'no doubt we'll find out what it's all about tonight.'

After twelve years together, I should have absorbed the simple philosophy that protected David from unnecessary stress. 'Don't cry now, wait and see if there is anything to cry about.' He was right, of course, but it didn't work for me. I lived in a constant state of fear and dread, which was only held in check by David's placid disposition.

David had showered and changed at work and was sitting in the lounge room watching television. He was laughing loudly at the outrageous antics of his favourite cartoon characters, when there was a knock on the door.

The woman introduced herself as Anna James and her companion as Nick somebody-or-other. Once they were seated at the dining-room table, I put the kettle on.

Anna was a very attractive woman in her early twenties. She wore no makeup, and she didn't need to – her skin was flawless. She had an unruly mass of shiny, black, curly hair that gave her a gypsy look.

Anna opened the conversation. 'As you can see I am pregnant, and the reason I am here is because I want to give the baby away.'

For a moment there was dead silence.

'Why?' David asked.

'I already have a two-year-old son, who is being reared by my mother,' Anna replied. 'She is old, I couldn't ask her to raise another child. And I am just not well enough, either, to care for a new baby.'

David was first to respond. 'I am flattered that you want to entrust your baby to us, but why? We are just ordinary working-class people; we don't have much to offer a child.'

'You have everything a child needs to grow up happy and healthy. I don't care if you aren't rich. I know that you and Audrey are loving and caring people, and that's all a child needs, to grow up with a strong body and a sound mind.'

I got the impression that Anna's own childhood had been lacking in these qualities. How else would someone so young have such deep insight into the needs of a child, unless they had experienced it first hand?

'You said you have a proposition,' David said. 'What do you want from us in return?' Anna stared long and hard into David's eyes and, for a moment, I wondered if she had heard him.

'I want nothing,' she said at last, 'except what I have already told you. I will make you a gift of my child in return for your solemn promise that you will love and care for the baby as you would your own.'

'How do we know that you won't want the baby later?' David asked.

'You don't know,' Anna replied. 'Just as I don't know if you will keep your end of the bargain. However, I give you my word that I will never intrude on your life again. We both have to go on our gut feeling that we can trust each other.'

Yasmin

When Anna James asked us if we would adopt her unborn child, I could not believe our good fortune. Because I was still married to Arnold, I had been living in this de facto relationship with David for twelve years, and all our efforts to have a child had met with failure. I had resigned myself to the fact that we would never have a child of our own.

So when we were offered this child, we accepted, without even discussing it with each other. Just a fleeting glance passed between us, and it was all the communication we needed to say, 'Yes, we would love to welcome your child, into our hearts and our home.'

We promised to take the child regardless of any mental or physical deficiencies he or she might have. We pledged to love and care for the child as long as we were able, together, or alone, whichever the case might be. This was an emotional time, as we sat at that table and plotted a way by which we could legally become the proud parents of Anna's boy or girl.

We had several meetings after that, and in that time we became good friends. I told Anna that David and I were not eligible to adopt children, because we were not legally married, and also we were too old. David was thirty-seven and I was thirty-nine.

'Doesn't matter, there are other ways,' Anna replied confidently.

I don't really remember who actually suggested that we switch identities. I think it just evolved from a number of choices. We made some outrageous suggestions, and we laughed till we cried. It was great fun.

Finally, we decided that we would go to Brisbane. Anna would enter the hospital as Audrey Evans and I would be her sister, Anna James. The baby would be registered to David and Audrey Evans.

∞

When Anna and I set out on our journey to find a birthplace for our child, Anna was eight months pregnant. We set off from Mount Isa in my new 1972 Holden Torana to drive to Brisbane. It was a long, hot, dusty trip, as the inland road was mostly unsealed. We left in the early hours of the morning, taking advantage of the cooler hours of the day to cover as much of our journey as possible before we would have to stop and rest.

At the next town, which was Kynuna, we rested and cooled down with several glasses of water, then we were on our way again. The journey of more than 1000 miles was barely started, and already we were feeling exhausted.

We spent the first night in Charleville, at the Country Women's Association hostel. It was plain, clean and comfortable and, best of all, affordable – just six dollars fifty a night each.

When we reached Brisbane, we made inquiries at two major hospitals, but were anxious about the amount of information they required. Because I was nearly twenty years older than Anna, we felt this information would betray us. We decided to return to a country town, where people might not pry so much.

Remember the angel

As we returned through Charleville and a little beyond, Anna began to experience labour pains. Not wanting to be caught in the 'never never' when the baby arrived, I turned the car around and headed back to Charleville. From my past experiences I have learned to listen to my inner voice and that voice was saying now, 'Remember the angel? Now it's time to put things right.' I don't know how much value to place on intuition, but it did seem strange that we had passed through Charleville twice already and were about to return to it a third time.

Had I known that my Aboriginal grandmother was born in Charleville, I would not have had any doubts. Nevertheless, even without this knowledge, I had to believe it was more than just coincidence that we were here at this time. I booked us both into the CWA hostel where we had stayed previously, then we went to the hospital. The doctor who examined Anna decided she wasn't due for at least another two weeks.

So we waited in Charleville.

During this time, I went to the cemetery to see if I could find the little grave. It had been thirty years since the angel had been washed away. Surprisingly, it was as if I had never been away: the cemetery looked almost the same, just a little older and more unkempt than I remembered. The old paling fence I used to climb through was still there, but time and the elements had taken their toll. The fence was now only half-standing, and in places had sagged all the way to the ground.

As I walked among the headstones, I felt a sense of belonging, like one who returns home after a long absence. I walked unerringly to the far corner of the graveyard, and there before me was the little grave. To me, it looked just the same, no more eroded and crumbling than the last time I had seen it. It was as if time had stood still, waiting for my return. As I paused there and looked back into the past, for one fleeting instant I saw again the angel at the base of the headstone. As if waking from a dream, I knew what I must do.

I was gripped by a sense of urgency. Hurriedly, I got into my car and returned to town. I found a shop that sold religious icons and bought an angel statuette similar to the one that was lost, and returned it to the small grave. As I rested the angel against the headstone, in almost the exact place where I had taken it from thirty years before, I felt a sense of relief sweep over me, like I had laid down a heavy burden instead of a tiny statuette. I had at last put another ghost to rest.

With a light heart and a lighter step, I returned to the hostel to await the birth of my very own angel.

18 March 1972

Several weeks later Anna went into labour, and when the time came for her to give birth, she was taken into the labour ward, where we continued our deception. Anna insisted that her 'sister' be allowed to stay with her throughout. It was a wonderful experience. Anna made hardly any sound despite her pain, the only evidence of her suffering an occasional low groan.

I watched my daughter come safely into the world, all buttered up and creamy, without a hint of the ordeal she had just been through. She was truly the most beautiful baby I had ever seen. Not so much as a wrinkle marred her flawless face.

The nurse went to give the baby to Anna but she said, 'No, I want my sister to hold her first.'

So I held my baby as if it were I who had given birth, and with tears in my eyes I said, 'Hello, Yasmin', and gently kissed her tiny forehead. Then I smiled and looked at Anna. Silently, I gave her thanks for this wonderful gift. She smiled back, and then we were both crying with happiness.

∞

Four days later I brought the car to the front steps of the hospital where Anna and the nurse carrying the baby were waiting. I got out to help Anna settle into the passenger seat, but she flew around to the driver's side and in behind the wheel, saying, 'I've been a passenger for too long, today I drive. Give the baby to her aunty.'

I got into the passenger seat and took the baby from the nurse.

I knew this was Anna's way of making me feel like Yasmin's mother, and I did feel like she was my own. She was just four days old and I loved her very much.

Anna was also very special to me. I believe the sacrifices she made to lay the foundations for a special bond to form between her baby and me were an example of pure, unselfish love. Anna knew she could not care for her child – she was unable to care for herself. Just as I was before I met David.

As I held my baby girl in my arms, it seemed I was gazing back through the corridors of time and I saw myself at seventeen with another four-day-old baby. I heard my mother and Matron Shaw trying to persuade me to give my baby up. To allow him to be adopted, and give him a chance to have a better start in life.

I was selfish. I wanted to keep him, and, ultimately, I ruined his life. Now I was being given a second chance, to love a child of my own, and I was determined I would not fail this time. I would make Anna proud of me and proud of her child.

Our deception had been successful: Yasmin was registered as the child of Audrey and David Evans, and nobody needed ever know the difference.

1972

They took my baby away

It was Friday 23 June and a man was standing on our front doorstep in Mount Isa. He identified himself to us as Mr North, resident childcare officer, from the Department of Children's Services.

'I believe you have a child in your care belonging to Anna James,' he said. 'I am here to take that child into State care, because we have reason to believe it has been abandoned.'

Another man appeared at the door. A detective.

I was suddenly very angry. 'What right do you have to enter my home and take my baby?' I demanded indignantly.

'We have information that you and the child's mother, Anna James, made false declarations on the registration forms.'

We realised that they knew everything. We discarded all pretence.

'Well, anyway, the baby has not been abandoned, she is in my care.' I spoke up bravely, but our world crumbled around us.

'I still have to take the baby,' Detective Lane insisted.

I played the only card we had left. 'Do you have a court warrant?'

He was unperturbed. 'No, but it'll only take Sergeant Price a few minutes to slip back to town and get one.'

I was puzzled. 'Who's Sergeant Price?'

Peter, who had been quietly watching the proceedings with David from the sidelines, said derisively, 'He's standing at the back door in case you make a run for it.'

I knew we had reached an impasse. Matters could only get worse. They were not going to leave without the baby, and we obviously had no legal claim to keep her. I felt the fight go out of me. Sadly I went into the nursery, picked up the sleeping child and for a moment held her close to my breast, one last time. I kissed her goodbye, thinking I would never see her again.

My heart was breaking as I handed Yasmin over to the childcare officer, and they all left quietly without another word. I wept then, the first of many bitter tears to follow. David was inconsolable, so I left him with his grief; it was as if our baby had died. But no one could have predicted the strange twist that would turn our lives around.

I was shaking as I dialled Anna's number. She answered with her comedy routine, as she often did with her friends: 'City Morgue, Anna Stiff speaking.'

'Anna,' I said, 'it's Audrey. Children's Services and the police have just taken Yasmin away, they said she had been abandoned and they were applying to have her made a ward of the State.' I heard Anna draw in her breath sharply.

'They can't do that, I can give my baby to anyone I please, there's no law against that.'

'I thought so too,' I said. 'But they know we changed names and they took her anyway. Anna, Yasmin is gone,' I sobbed.

∞

The next day Anna and I visited Mr North, of the Children's Services. Anna asked why he had removed the baby from my care. He said he had received information that Anna had given her baby to a woman who was mentally deranged, and the baby had been taken into State care to insure its safety. 'Of course,' North said, 'I know now that's not true. Nevertheless, the baby will not be returned to David and Audrey Evans because they are not married.'

'I'll fight you,' Anna said.

North shrugged. 'You can apply to the court to regain custody of Yasmin, but the case will not be heard until next Friday 30 June at 10 a.m.'

'I'll be there,' Anna said grimly.

Later that day, as David, Anna and I talked about getting Yasmin back, Anna said, 'They are obviously not going to give Yasmin back to you and Dave, so it's up to me. My solicitor said to bring you to the court on Friday because you can act as a character witness for me. He said that they couldn't keep Yasmin. They have no legal grounds . . . but listen here, you two,' Anna said sternly to David and me, 'there is obviously someone in this town who doesn't want you to have this baby. So as soon as the court gives her back to me, I want you both to take the baby and get out of town, and tell no one where you are going, okay?'

David and I agreed.

The court case

On Friday morning, although I was to take no part in the case, except to act as a character witness for Anna, I dressed carefully. I wore my best black fitted dress, which was smart yet conservative. My hair was well groomed, and dark glasses concealed my reddened eyes. When I was ready, I kissed David goodbye and looked into his sad face.

Poor David, he had suffered so much since they took Yasmin away, my heart ached for him.

At the Mount Isa courthouse, where the case was being heard, I met with Mr Southers, the solicitor, and Anna. Then we entered the courtroom, which was empty save for Mr North, who sat alone at a desk on the right. There was nothing about him that would make him stand out in a crowd. He was middle-aged, of medium height and build. His hair was a dark sandy colour. His eyes were of an indeterminate colour. In fact, I wondered how such an insignificant person could wield so much power over people's lives.

Mr North stated his case first. He wanted to make an application to make Yasmin Camille Evans a ward of the State, on the grounds of information received that a person who was mentally ill, mentally unstable and mentally deranged had in her care a young baby that had been abandoned by its mother for three months. There was a great deal more, but finally he said how, with the assistance of Detective Lane and Sergeant Price, he had seized the child from Mrs Evans because he believed the baby was at risk.

'Is Mrs Evans in the courtroom now?' the judge asked.

'Yes, your Honour, she is sitting on the left of Mr Southers.' He pointed to me.

The judge, who was sitting directly in front of me, peered over his eyeglasses at me for a long minute, then turned to Mr North and asked bluntly, 'Well, is Mrs Evans mentally deranged?'

'No, your Honour, we have since proved this accusation to be untrue.'

In response Mr Southers said that the childcare officer had acted illegally, impulsively, irrationally and was out of line.

Then it was the judge's turn to speak. 'I do not know why this case is before me,' he said. 'I see it as a civil action between two women who, by the way, do not have any disagreement. I refuse to rule in this case, and suggest if you wish to continue, you take it to the Supreme Court at four o'clock today.'

Before we knew it Anna and I were outside standing at the top of the courtroom steps, looking down in amazement at Detective Lane, Mr Southers, and Mr North, yelling, swearing, waving their arms about, and generally having an unholy row. Anna looked at me.

'Did we start all that?'

It was over. Mr North stood before me and said, 'You come with me, I want to talk to you alone.'

He led me down under the courthouse near the toilet block and said in a low voice, 'There is no way I am going to give this baby back to her mother. She has abandoned it, and I have no reason to believe she will not do so again. However, I will agree to let you have the child provided you promise never to take any court action against anybody connected with this case, now or ever.'

'Yes, yes,' I said. 'I agree, I only want my baby back.'

'Wait here,' he said, and Detective Lane and Mr Southers each asked me to make the same promise, which I did.

It was settled.

I accompanied Mr North to his office in the Department of Children's Services, and signed a form giving David and me full legal custody of Yasmin Camille Evans.

Later I discovered that Mr North was open to a lawsuit by David and me for wrongful removal of a child in our care. So the return of the child, and our agreeing not to prosecute, averted this.

1974

Will you love my baby too?

Yasmin was just two years old when another young girl came to our door and introduced herself simply as Maria. She told us that she was only fifteen years old and was still at school – 'and as you can see I am very pregnant.'

She said, 'I have heard what kind and caring parents you are and how much you love your own little girl, and I wondered if you could find it in your heart to love my child too.'

I told Maria that Yasmin was also adopted, and that her child was very welcome. She was eight months pregnant and my heart went out to her. I recalled my own experience as a young, pregnant teenager.

So, on 16 May, we received a telephone call from Maria to come to the hospital to see our new son.

He was beautiful. I was sure Maria would change her mind and decide to keep him.

But four days later Maria brought the baby to our house, and asked us to name him before she gave him up for good. We named him Jason David, and we were unable to believe we had been blessed with yet another wonderful child.

∞

These children changed my life. I gave up drinking and smoking and became a dedicated mother. I loved my children with an intensity that made me perhaps a little more protective than was good for them. Nevertheless, I wanted us to be a family – not divided into parents and children, but a close family unit. I encouraged the children to be kind, loving and understanding of David and each other. Of course, this didn't always work; each child had their own distinct personality, and fights and tantrums were common. However, as soon as the anger was spent, the family was there offering support and forgiveness for the wayward family member. 'After all,' we would say, 'we all stuff up sometimes, it's no big deal.' David and I had little experience in raising children, so when Yasmin had been born I bought a book on the subject. But when the author advised parents to tie a fishing net over the child's cot to prevent them from climbing out, I threw the book away, and thereafter used my own common sense.

1975: two kids, two cats and a caravan

A year later we left Mount Isa. Peter decided to stay behind, so we set off with two kids and two cats and travelled by car and caravan, doing seasonal work. We picked potatoes and onions in Gatton in south-east Queensland. There was stone fruit in Stanthorpe, and potatoes in Guyra and Dorrigo in New South Wales. And finally we settled in a cotton-growing town in New South Wales near Narrabri. The main reason for Wee Waa's existence was its cotton industry.

When David began work on the cotton farms, he was told of the floods that Wee Waa had endured for years. Many farmers, unable to make a living due to the constant flooding, left the area. However, those who stayed invested time and money into a plan to hold back the water. They built high levees that surrounded the cotton fields on every farm. These embankments were designed to hold back the floodwaters, which threatened to destroy the crops each year. Somehow, they were never quite high enough. Each year the waters rose just that little bit more.

Our house was built flat on the ground on a concrete slab. The house grounds were most inhospitable. Hot, dusty and covered in bindies and burrs. There were also poisonous biting creatures in abundance. Snakes, huge spiders, scorpions and ants that caused excruciating pain if you were bitten. To give us some protection we all wore rubber boots outside the house. In spite of this, we were happy there. While I enjoyed the peace and solitude of country living, my health improved. The kids loved the open spaces. No fences within 'cooee', as David used to say.

By this time Peter had married a seventeen-year-old called Carmen, a girl he had known since childhood. When their first child, Deborah, was born on 21 July 1975, they were unsettled and moving around looking for work. The baby was just three weeks old when I offered to care for her until they settled down.

By then I had three children under five years old. Yasmin was three, Jason was one, and Debbie was three weeks. Over the next six years Debbie lived with us part of the time as well as with her parents, until finally, when she had to start school, it was decided she would stay with David and me, and the children she had grown up with.

Part Five

1978, Aged 45

Something is wrong with David

David and I had some difficult years. We were living in Margate on the Redcliffe Peninsula when first I noticed that something was wrong with David. He would hit his head whenever he went under the house to collect wood for the combustion stove. No matter how many times he hit his head, he never learned to duck.

Three large bumps had to be surgically removed from his head. The doctor advised me that David had suffered some form of brain damage from the leptospirosis. He suggested that to avoid further damage he should wear a crash helmet, or alternatively move to a lower- or higher-set house. We moved and the problem of David's head was solved, but not the underlying cause.

Nevertheless, perhaps because of money or because of the difficulties we were having, David went north for three years to work in a uranium mine until the mine closed.

Soon after this, David's legs began to swell until they resembled large tree stumps and he found it difficult to walk, climb stairs and even sleep at night. Back in Brisbane the doctors diagnosed David's condition as elephantiasis of the legs.

I altered his trouser legs to accommodate the swelling and this made his clothes more comfortable to wear.

But then he began to have a series of mild strokes. As the strokes became more severe and more frequent, a CAT scan revealed that David had suffered irreversible brain damage.

David's health and mental condition continued to deteriorate over the years. Even so he never lost his sense of humour. Each time I took him to hospital, he partially recovered and came home.

Then one night David went to hospital and never came home again.

2 July 1987
My best chance at love

The night David died began no differently from any other night.

As usual, Jason was the first to go to bed, around eight-thirty. Yasmin and I sat up and watched television together. Debbie wasn't living with us at this time; she had returned to her family for an extended holiday.

It was around ten o'clock when David complained of a severe headache. I gave him two aspirin with a glass of water, and he returned to bed. A short time later, I heard the toilet door squeaking as it did when it was opened and shut. I called to David, asking him if he was all right, but when he didn't answer I went to investigate. I found David sitting on the toilet, naked except for his boxer shorts around his ankles. He was barely conscious.

I called to Yasmin to ring an ambulance, and after making the call, she came to help me.

I knew we had to get David off the toilet and onto the floor, but he was a big man and too heavy for us to hold. When I asked David to try to stand up he said, 'I can't.' And these were the last words David ever spoke. The one person who had taught me how to survive was now losing his own battle to live.

By the time the ambulancemen arrived David had slipped off the seat and was wedged tightly between the toilet and the wall. He was dying. When the ambulancemen got David onto the stretcher, Yasmin noticed a towel was caught underneath him. She tried to pull the towel out but it wouldn't budge. I was about to tell Yassy to leave it, when David suddenly opened his eyes, sat up, lifted himself up and pulled the towel out from under him. He handed it to Yasmin and then lay down again and slipped into a coma.

∞

David was taken to hospital, where he was placed on life-support. The next day the doctor told me that David was brain-dead, and asked my permission to turn off the life support system and allow him to die naturally.

As I stood beside the hospital bed and held David's hand, I couldn't help thinking how well he looked. His skin was a healthy pink colour and he felt warm to the touch. He didn't look or feel dead.

Nevertheless, at 3.15 on 3 July 1987, I said a last goodbye to David. As the machine was turned off I felt the deepest sense of loss. I was overcome with the greatest sadness at losing the only person who had ever loved me, and the only true friend I had ever had.

David's death touched us all in different ways. We supported each other in our grief. We cried in each other's arms and consoled each other. Significantly, at this time I recalled my mother's death and how four young girls grieved alone, in their separate cubbyholes. And my father's death, when I grieved alone as our father passed away.

Peter was handling his grief in his own way. He was so devastated when he was told that David was dying, he couldn't come to the hospital. It was just too hard for him to say goodbye to the only father he had ever known and loved. But David knew and understood Peter better than any of us, and before his life support system was turned off David visited Peter.

Peter told me that he was sitting alone in the lounge room of my home crying as he thought how much David had wanted him to call him Dad. For some reason he had felt he couldn't say it although he wanted to. He wished he had. He knew it would have made David so happy and now it was too late. Then he felt great calm come over him and he wasn't hurting any more. He raised his head and saw David sitting in the armchair facing him. David was smiling and Peter said, 'What are you doing here? I thought you were in the hospital.' Peter wasn't alarmed in any way. Nor did he think it strange when David didn't answer. But after several minutes David got to his feet, and Peter said, 'Where are you going?' David simply said 'Home' – then the phone rang, and I told Peter that David had died.

Moving On

David and I had been together for twenty-seven years. Three days before he died we had signed a contract to move into a larger house, as our two-bedroom dwelling was too small for our family of five. The three kids had to sleep in bunkbeds in the one room. Our new house, which was only a couple of streets away from where we had been living, had five bedrooms, three upstairs and two downstairs. David saw the house only once and he loved it, but he died before we were able to move in.

I was very angry at this time. I was angry at being poor and with David for leaving me. I was angry with myself for being weak and irrational. Yet it was anger that kept me going through times of utter despair. Anger was the driving force that enabled me to carry on without David.

The contract for our new house allowed us to move in without paying the bond of $440 upfront. But we had to pay a weekly rate of $110 rent plus $110 off the bond. With the added $1000 debt for David's funeral, I knew I could not manage unless I found work quickly.

Because I was in my fifties, and because I was uneducated and unskilled, I could only expect to get the most menial, low-paid jobs. First I took a job delivering groceries for a Brisbane Cash and Carry Foodstore at $2.50 per order. That was a disaster. In the first week, I left all the cold food behind in the store's freezer and had to make a second delivery to each house. Then I left an order of six boxes in a carport and the family dog was chomping on a leg of lamb when the customer returned fifteen minutes later. I had failed to read the fine print, *Do not deliver until 3 p.m.*

Finally, one rainy day as I was going down a very long flight of wet stairs, I slipped and slid all the way to the bottom on my back, my head bumping on every step. I didn't break anything, but I was bruised and grazed. I decided there had to be better jobs and I advertised a pick-up and delivery ironing service at five dollars an hour. Before long I had more work than I could handle. However, after a few weeks my legs and feet swelled and pained so badly, I had to stand on a pillow while I ironed. I tried various other jobs but somehow I couldn't seem to get it right. When I took a job cleaning a house at nine dollars an hour, I accidentally let the prize cat out and it was run over by a car.

The Sweet Life

Jason 13, Yasmin 15, Debbie 12

One day as I was looking through the local paper for more suitable work, I saw an advertisement for children to sell lollies to support the Cystic Fibrosis Foundation. I rang the contact number and Yassy and Jason were hired, but Debbie was too young, too timid and too scared to do this kind of work.

The next day the supervisor, Keith, picked up the children at four o'clock and took them to an area where they were to sell their lollies. It didn't dawn on me until after they had left that I had just let my children go with a strange man in his car. I knew nothing about him, I had only answered an advertisement in the newspaper.

I had a phone number that might or might not be genuine and having imagined all sorts of terrible things that could have happened to Jason and Yassy, I picked up the phone and dialled the number. I didn't really expect anyone to answer, and agonised over the fact that I had fallen for the oldest trick of all – *a man with a bag of lollies.*

I couldn't believe it when somebody picked up the phone and a soft, woman's voice answered. For a moment I was unable to speak, my throat was thick and dry.

'Hello,' I finally croaked. 'My two children started selling lollies with Keith today.'

I paused, expecting her to say, 'Who's Keith?' But to my relief she said, 'Yes, my husband told me he was picking up two new children from Coopers Plains.'

'Oh,' I said lamely. 'I was just checking, ah, um, to see what time they would be home.'

This work earned the children thirty cents for every two-dollar bag of lollies they sold. Although the money was good, when I found out they were left alone on street corners up until nine o'clock at night, I applied for the job of supervisor. In this position, I drove the car, following the kids around. It gave me control of the hours they worked and I made sure they were never left alone again.

I guess Debbie got tired of sitting in the car refilling the baskets as Yasmin and Jason returned with theirs empty and, after hearing the tales they related of funny or sad things they had seen and heard, she decided she wanted a piece of the action. So Debbie, along with Yasmin's school friend Kaylene, made up our new team of very efficient lolly sellers. In the New Year we decided to strike out on our own.

Our cottage industry

Having learned the mechanics of the business, we were now

skilled enough to start our own 'cottage industry', as we preferred to call it. The buying, packing, marketing, and selling of confectionery gave the children valuable knowledge, and multiple skills. They learnt to buy only top-quality brands and to check for freshness; they acquired skills in weights and measures, food hygiene, presentation, packaging, labelling and stock rotation.

For example, the containers or tubs for the lollies were the first, most important factor. They should be transparent, airtight and the right size. A small container crammed with 200g of lollies appeared to be better value than a larger container, only half full, although the weight and quantity were the same. The sizes, shape, texture and colour of the lollies were important factors in whether or not people would buy our product.

'Children want the tubs with more colourful lollies,' Debbie and Yasmin agreed, 'but older folk more often choose the darker shades.'

'Yes,' Jason said nodding wisely, 'but teenagers examine every tub looking for the one with the most lollies.'

We all laughed, because every tub had an equal amount.

Above all, they learnt a lot about people and themselves. They learned how to handle rejection, to recognise that the customer was rejecting the lollies, not themselves personally. They learned self-control and how to smile and be polite no matter how rude the client was. Most importantly, our cottage industry kept the kids out of trouble and, ironically, 'off the streets'. The following year we were financially better off, so we gave up the lolly business to concentrate on school studies.

Educational studies

Ever since David's death, I had been afraid of living in poverty in my old age, or worse, of ending up a 'bag lady' on the railway station. Now I had come to realise that I was not going to be able to continue doing manual work into my old age. Yet I was not trained to do anything else.

Although my educational skills were limited, I tried working as a voluntary teacher-aide at the Oxley Secondary College. For nine months I worked there, helping kids to read and write. It was at this time I realised that if I studied for the year-twelve Senior Certificate, the Queensland equivalent of the High School Certificate (HSC), I could possibly get a job as a tutor or teacher-aide.

So in 1988, I enrolled in the year-twelve adult education Senior Certificate at Oxley Secondary College in Brisbane. Throughout the year, I did well in all subjects, especially English, where I excelled in Shakespeare and poetry. Unfortunately, when I sat for the examination at the end of the year, I suffered a mental blackout. I couldn't recall anything that I had learned all year, not even the name of the Shakespearean play I loved so much. When I received a mark of low achievement, I was devastated.

Nevertheless, with encouragement from my teacher, Mary Henley, I repeated the subject the following year and received a mark of Sound Achievement which got me a place at Griffith University in Brisbane in 1990. I began a Bachelor of Arts Degree, majoring in Comparative Studies in History and Literature. Three years later I graduated, and as I walked across the stage wearing the blue academic gown and mortarboard of Griffith University, it was one of the most exciting days of my life.

Spurred on by my initial success I undertook further study at Griffith University, and in 1995 got a Graduate Diploma of Adult and Vocational Education, qualifying me as a primary and secondary school teacher. I didn't feel emotionally secure enough to teach full time, so I registered as a classroom supply teacher with the Education Department. As a supply teacher, I received only an hour or less notice to be at whichever school I was required at. It was quite an experience to teach in these modern times because although I was now the teacher instead of the student, I still got the short end of the stick. Students now had more legal rights than the teacher.

The cane and the rap over the knuckles with the ruler had been abolished, along with all forms of corporal punishment. Not that I approved of those barbaric methods of behaviour management, but it was helpful sometimes to know they were there.

I decided to write down some of my experiences, so that I could better understand what had happened to me and why, in the hope that it would better equip me to deal with the aftermath. While I reflected on my traumatic past and subsequent achievements, I hoped that by writing my story, others too might know how much could be achieved if one was prepared to work hard and have faith in oneself.

1990s

It was at this time that I received a phone call from Lynne Schonefeld, the field officer for the Aboriginal Tutoring Assistance Scheme (ATAS), where I was under contract as a tutor. She said, 'I wondered, Audrey, if you would be interested in an unusual tutoring assignment.' Without waiting for my reply she went on, 'I have a student who has very special needs and I thought of you straight away. This person needs a kind and caring person who is also skilled in adult education, and I know you have these qualities.'

I was very puzzled. I had been registered with ATAS for three years and several times in the past I had been contracted to tutor clients with both mental and physical disabilities. But this time it was different. The strange rippling sensation went through my body which usually meant 'Take care!'

Lynne explained that she needed a tutor for an inmate of the Wolston Park Mental Hospital, formerly called Goodna

Mental Hospital. I went cold. I felt a trickle down my spine; there was a loud roaring in my ears. I had spent the best part of my young life going in and out of there.

Lynne was still talking but I couldn't hear what she was saying. Suddenly my knees gave way and I sat down heavily on a chair. I heard Lynne say, 'You don't have to take this job. If you don't want to I will understand.'

Taking my silence to mean I was undecided, Lynne said, 'Look, why don't we leave it for the moment? I'll call you again in the morning around ten o'clock and you can give me your answer then.'

Lynne could not have known the enormity of what she was asking. She knew nothing of my past history and she certainly didn't know of the years I had spent in the same establishment. All that day I tried to come to terms with my fears. What if I did go back into that 'house of horrors', that monster that swallowed people whole? It sucked out all hope of ever being released: 'You are in here for good, madam, and you had better behave, because we have ways of dealing with those who cause us trouble.'

It bled you dry of all things that made you a person, an identity. All self-respect, all feelings of self-worth and self-esteem were stripped away and you were no longer able to make decisions about your own person. You became grey-faced, lifeless, brainless: in fact, institutionalised. Then the monster would shit you out the back door onto the street, your papers stamped *Recovered*.

That night you'd sleep with a fellow in return for a bed and a couple of quid to buy brandy. The police would pick you up the next day for being drunk and you'd be returned to the monster and it would start all over again. Your papers would once more be stamped, not drunk but *Schizophrenic*.

I tossed and turned all night and eventually decided that, if I could mentally walk through the hospital and come out reasonably unscathed, I would accept Lynne's offer.

I had to force myself in my mind to walk slowly and not give in to the instinctive fear to turn and run away. Run, not from the unknown but from the very real fear of losing my mind.

I knew that this was my best opportunity to come face to face with the ghosts of the past. In my mind I boldly walked through the reception rooms. Adopting a nonchalant air, I stopped to smell the fresh flowers in glass vases and to admire the framed pictures on the wall. There were pastoral scenes of idyllic landscapes, and still-life paintings of the inevitable bowls of fruit. But I knew these rooms were the only place that bore any semblance of normality in the whole establishment.

The staff who greeted new and mildly affected patients were friendly and gracious. They called you by your name, even inquiring, 'Er, Miss? Mrs?' With eyebrows raised, they waited for your reply. The important thing here was that you still had your identity. Your own name, your own face, your own thoughts and your own particular smell. Regardless of how good or bad it was, it was still essentially yours. You still had that old favourite jumper – that you insisted on bringing – the one that even your dog recognised as yours. Importantly, you were still you. You hadn't yet been absorbed into the melting pot, the institutional dung heap.

After going down several long corridors and passing through locked doors, I imagined I was standing in one of the smaller wards where there were only about six beds. In that part of the hospital your mental health was assessed. After a few days there, depending on the doctor's findings, you would be allocated to a dormitory.

Really, I had such negative thoughts of this place that I'd forgotten how nice those reception wards were. The floral drapes hanging at the windows were of cotton cretonne. They were looped back and fastened with tiebacks of the same material. The walls were of a light pastel shade of no definable colour. The ceilings were high, which added to the illusion that the rooms were light and airy and larger than they actually were.

The beds were covered with whiter-than-white coverlets, whiter even than bleached bones in a desert. They were perfectly embroidered with large red poinsettias. Some people, including myself, saw these coverlets as beautiful works of art. Others complained that the red flowers with their long thin red petals looked like someone had been stabbed and bled to death on the white coverlet.

There was an old hospital superstition that when red and white flowers were brought into the ward it meant someone was going to die. I recalled also that those bed covers were worked by some of the inmates as part of their occupational therapy. In those clean, neat rooms there was an appearance of industrious normality, of people getting well and going home after a week or two. But this too was an illusion.

Simply because there was an unusually large turnover of patients constantly passing through those rooms it cannot be argued that any one of them went home. They were simply transferred to other, less opulent parts of the hospital.

Nevertheless, there was certainly an expectation of hope in that area of the hospital, a hope that gradually diminished as I penetrated deeper into this institution of pain, fear and human suffering.

As you walked through the hospital you noticed how the perspective changed. Going from loose white covers to grey blankets there was the feeling that the beds were constrained in tight little grey straitjackets, matching the inmates' faces and skin.

There was another ward yet, the refractory ward. There was a big gate into a yard the size of a tennis court, all bitumen, no shade: the bad ones were put in there. I had the soles of my feet burnt in that yard. Down at the very end of the 'courtyard' were rooms like jail cells. The noisy and violent ones were kept in there, because they screamed all night. They only had a mattress and a pot. They were kept in solitary all the time and would never be released. The warden went there every morning and opened the door, and every morning the girl threw the pee pot at him and every morning she was belted up, by the warders.

That was my greatest fear – that I would one day end up like that.

∞

When Lynne rang me the following morning, I had already made up my mind that I would return to the hospital and face my fears. Now, as she parked the car and we walked towards Noble House, where we were to visit Lauren, I slipped and fell heavily, one leg twisted underneath me.

An accident? Or an unconscious attempt to delay or prevent me from entering the place I feared so much?

Apart from bruising and slight gravel-rash I was not hurt. But it was enough to make me realise that I must tell Lynne the truth about my connection with the hospital.

Lynne seemed to already sense my agitation and uncertainty. She didn't know the real reason but I knew she thought that I was afraid of dealing with a mental patient.

I had to explain to Lynne that I was not afraid of Lauren, but of the institution itself.

'Lynne,' I said, 'could I have a few minutes to talk before we go in?'

'Of course,' she replied. 'But, Audrey, we don't have to go in if you don't want to. We can just go back to the car and go home. I realise this is a very difficult assignment and I will understand if you would rather not do it.'

How kind and understanding Lynne was. And for that reason too I felt I owed her an explanation. Standing there outside the red brick building of Noble House, I confided to Lynne that I had been a mental patient in this same hospital. As I spoke I saw a series of emotions pass across her face. At first there was surprise, then disbelief, followed by pity. Then, as Lynne struggled to regain her composure, I saw her eyes shining with respect and admiration, and I knew I was right to tell her the truth.

'Oh, Audrey, how awful for you,' Lynne exclaimed. 'I'm so sorry . . . if I had only known . . .'

'No, Lynne,' I said firmly. 'You mustn't blame yourself. It was my decision to accept the assignment, and I did so because I felt I had at last been given an opportunity to put to rest a ghost that has haunted me ever since I was an inmate here almost forty years ago.' I smiled with forced bravado. 'Shall we go in?'

But I was anything but brave when we went through the front door. We went first to an office where Lynne introduced me to a man in a blue suit. Lynne shook hands with him, but I didn't. I half expected him to grab me by the arm and throw me in a cell. I was acutely aware of my whole body trembling. I gripped my hands tightly together so he wouldn't notice. However, my fear subsided when the ringing of the telephone abruptly terminated our meeting and, with a slight nod of his head, we were dismissed.

A nursing staff member led us through several doors which she unlocked, and we eventually entered a pleasant garden enclosure. As we left the covered verandah with the cement floor, we moved across the neat lawn area to a wooden outdoor setting, where an Aboriginal woman was seated.

'That's Lauren,' Lynne murmured softly. I saw that Lauren was a tall, powerfully built woman of about forty-five. I was intrigued by the cruel set of her mouth in an otherwise attractive face. And by the aura of mystery I sensed about her. I searched Lauren's dark, smoky, almost black eyes for the wounded child within, looking for some common ground, an affinity each inmate has with a fellow human being.

At first I saw nothing. However, I put this down to Lauren being unwilling to meet my eyes. Her eyes flitted from one person to another, never actually coming to rest on any individual. When I attempted to gain her attention by asking her a direct question, she lowered her heavy dark lashes, effectively shutting out me and the rest of the world. It was an action that brought back haunting memories of my own stay in this institution, of my attempts to protect my own private person.

At the end of our visit Lauren decided that she didn't want to study at that time, and, as far as Lynne was concerned, our visit had been fruitless. But for me it had been an intensely rewarding experience because, although bad memories of the hospital would always remain, they would no longer be hidden in the deep recesses of my mind. The ghosts of Goodna Mental Hospital had finally been exorcised.

Epilogue

by Yasmin Evans

The most important words a child can ever write are the epilogue to their mother's book. It is a great honour and responsibility to have the last word on her life, as she was the true storyteller. The book begins with Mum graduating from Griffith University and it ends with her facing her fears at Wolston Park Hospital. This, however, was not the final chapter in her life; in fact it was only the beginning. Mum was passionate about education and creating a better life for her children. After graduating from her first degree she went on to complete a postgraduate degree in Education. I remember the struggle she faced, with many of her lecturers saying that she was too old to start teaching, but in true Audrey fashion, she qualified as a teacher the same year she qualified for the old age pension. While most people her age were planning their retirement, Mum was writing lesson plans. We often discussed how many people failed to see the importance of Aboriginal Elders in the education system and the impact they could have on guiding future generations. Mum understood this need and had a burning passion to help change the direction of the lives of many Indigenous people.

In 1999 she received the NAIDOC Indigenous Scholar of the Year Award for her contribution to teaching and assisting Indigenous students to go on to tertiary study. I recall one student's funny story of how she met Mum and Mum encouraged her to undertake further study. The Aboriginal woman was sitting in a hospital waiting room, dressed in a hospital gown and waiting for a breast scan. Mum was there for the same reason. Mum immediately introduced herself and they started talking and sharing their stories while they waited for the doctor to come. The woman was shocked to discover that Mum had returned to study at such a late age, and confessed that she had always wanted to but was scared. Mum, in her hospital gown, smiled at her and said, 'I'll show you how.' A few months later the woman was enrolled in an Education course at Australian Catholic University.

Continuing to lead us by example, Mum carried on with her education, enrolling in a Master of Arts in Creative Writing, with her autobiography as her main thesis. Australian Catholic University also offered her a part-time job lecturing in Indigenous Culture as part of their education course. Mum's painful history fuelled her desire to educate people and develop new ways of dealing with difference.

Mum also began teaching at high schools and at child detention centres; she loved working with the kids the education system forgot and giving them emotional support. As an Elder, she was a strong presence in many of these children's lives; she was often the only 'parent' they had known. Adopting children was not a big deal; it was what she thought everyone should do. We always had other kids living with us as we grew up. One of my strongest memories was of two small children turning up on our doorstep one night in their pyjamas. They had run away from a children's home and had heard from another child that Mrs Evans was a good lady who would look after them. Mum took them in, fed them and put them to bed. We were amazed at how they had managed to run away and catch a bus and train in their pyjamas and nobody had stopped them. It broke Mum's heart the next day when she had to ring the children's home and let them know they were with us.

I believe my mother first began writing her story as a type of therapy. It was her way of piecing together the memories of what had happened and a search for the reasons why they had happened. Before she found this outlet, she was an incredibly angry woman who went from one drama to another. As a child I witnessed many angry outbursts and the chronic depression that always followed. I was perplexed by Mum's incredible strength when she was arguing with someone (often someone at Social Security) and her child-like nature when she was depressed. As she progressed with her writing, Mum began sharing her story with me. Slowly, I began to understand why she was such a contradiction. It took ten years for her to write and share her story with her family. Her biggest fear was that her children would reject her and be ashamed of her. Mum couldn't have been more wrong. We all loved her deeply and it was by sharing her story with us that we were able to understand our family better. I told her this, but at the time I never realised just how important her book would be in bonding her children together.

On Christmas Day 2000, Mum died from a stroke. The shock that overwhelmed our family is still felt today. When I found her body in her housing commission house at Acacia Ridge it was hard to comprehend that the woman who had been the strongest person I had ever known was gone. It was after the ambulance had taken her body away that I found her completed manuscript sitting on the kitchen table in a box clearly marked. The house was very messy, but Mum had made sure that I would easily find her book. It had taken ten years to write and she had completed it a few weeks before she died. Over those years Mum had become a calmer, more centred person. The book was the constant theme in her life. At Mum's funeral her children made a promise that we would publish her work no matter what it took. Well, Mum, we kept our promise.

Acknowledgements

This book has taken sixteen years to be published and Audrey's family would like to acknowledge and thank the following people:

All the Aboriginal Elders of this land who continue to share their spirit, wisdom and hope with their people and communities.

Judith Lukin-Amundsen, for being a mentor to our mother and agreeing to edit this book.

Our sister in spirit, Leah Purcell, for her wonderful insight and words of inspiration.

Professor Carole Ferrier and Jan McKemmish (School of English, Media Studies and Art History, University of Queensland) for their supervision and support when Mum was completing her Master of Arts in Creative Writing at the University of Queensland. For their personal and professional commitment: Sam Watson, Hilary Beaton, Vanessa Whitelaw, Mary Graham, and others, who, at the

Queensland Writers Centre, produced the Indigenous Mentorship Program; later they also gained funding from Arts Queensland for ongoing work on and support of the manuscript *Many Lifetimes*.

To all her students, family and friends who encouraged our mum to share her story.

Official Documents From Goodna Mental Hospital

MEDICAL CERTIFICATE

In the matter of AUDREY MAY ▮▮▮▮ an alleged mentally sick person.

4. I formed this conclusion on the following grounds, viz.:—

(i.) Facts indicating mental sickness observed by myself at the time of the said examination, viz.:

Very depressed woman; says everything is hopeless and has no plans for future. Says she wants to die.

Suicidal.
Not dangerous.

(ii.) Facts indicating mental sickness communicated to me by others.

Name and address of person communicating facts:

SISTER ▮▮▮▮
BRISBANE HOSPITAL.

Facts communicated:

WARD CONDUCT: Sullen; depressed.
Food;   Poor
Habits;   Clean
Violence;   Nil here
Suicidal ideas; Yes.

Sgd. ▮▮▮▮

MEDICAL CERTIFICATE

In the matter of AUDREY MAY ▮▮▮▮ an alleged mentally sick person.

4. I formed this conclusion on the following grounds, viz.:—

    (i.) Facts indicating mental sickness observed by myself at the time of the said examination, viz.:

She appears vague and depressed and displays no interest or activity. She has no immediate plans regarding herself and gives an unsatisfactory history of her past activities.

Not Suicidal.
Not Dangerous.

    (ii.) Facts indicating mental sickness communicated to me by others.

Name and address of person communicating facts:
    SISTER ▮▮▮▮
    BRISBANE HOSPITAL.

Facts communicated:

    WARD CONDUCT: Sullen; depressed.
    FOOD: Poor
    HABITS: Clean
    VIOLENCE: Nil here
    Sucidal ideas; Yes.

                                         Sgd. ▮▮▮▮▮▮▮▮

RE-ADMITTED
MEDICAL CERTIFICATE

In the matter of ▬▬▬▬ known as Audrey May an alleged mentally sick person.

4. I formed this conclusion on the following grounds, viz.:—

(i.) Facts indicating mental sickness observed by myself at the time of the said examination, viz.:

Frequent mood swings.
Depressed.
Talking of suicide.

Suicidal.
Not Dangerous.

(ii.) Facts indicating mental sickness communicated to me by others.

Name and address of person communicating facts:

Sister ▬▬▬▬
Brisbane Hospital.

Facts communicated:

Ward Conduct: Agitated. Depressed, Tried to hang herself.
Food: Fair.
Habits: Clean.
Violence: Nil,
Suicidal Ideas: Yes.

Signed:- ▬▬▬▬ Brisbane

MEDICAL CERTIFICATE

In the matter of ▮▮▮▮ Audrey May an alleged mentally sick person.

4. I formed this conclusion on the following grounds, viz.:—

    (i.) Facts indicating mental sickness observed by myself at the time of the said examination, viz:

She is restless and imagines she can hear her mother's voice ou the room. She has attempted to strangle herself twice since ir Hospital. Can give no account of herself. No insight into mer state.

    (ii.) Facts indicating mental sickness communicated to me by others.

Name and address of person communicating facts:

SISTER ▮▮▮▮
BRISBANE HOSPITAL.

Facts communicated:

                      SAME AS ON ABOVE CERTIFICATE.

                                  (SGD) ▮▮▮▮

                                        5:12:'52.

MEDICAL CERTIFICATE

In the matter of ▇▇▇ Audrey May ▇▇ an alleged mentally sick person.

4. I formed this conclusion on the following grounds, viz.:—

(i.) Facts indicating mental sickness observed by myself at the time of the said examination, viz.:

She is flippant in manner and completely irresponsible in her statements. Says she wants to get drunk and likes to drink.

(ii.) Facts indicating mental sickness communicated to me by others.

Name and address of person communicating facts:
SISTER ▇▇▇
    BRISBANE HOSPITAL.

Facts communicated:

Ward Conduct:	Sings loudly, sees and talks to people no present.
Food:	Good.
Habits:	Clean.
Violence:	Aggressive on admission.
Suicidal Ideas:	Attempted suicide twice by strangling.

(SGD) ▇▇▇ 5:12:

BRISBANE

GOODNA: February 19, 54.

JA:L

The Director of Social Services,
 Family Allowances Branch,
  Commonwealth Offices,
   Anzac Square,
   BRISBANE. B9.

Dear Sir,

        Re : AUDREY M.

        Your letter of the 17th instant to hand, ref. C3/202206 NLM and in reply thereto I have to advise that the abovenamed patient was admitted to this Hospital on the 13th October, 1953 and provisional diagnosis was Schizophrenia.

        The patient has not responded well to treatment and her stay here will probably be lengthy.

                              Yours faithfully,

                              MEDICAL SUPERINTENDENT.

Miss A. M. ▓
"Ringorah"
Warren N.S.W.
22-5-55

Dear Dr ▓,

I am writing this in reference to my discharge papers as I have not received any. Also I have been in contact with Mr ▓ who also claims he has not received any either. Mr ▓ is my friend who took me at the time of my discharge.

I have some valuables in the Public Curator's which I doubt I can claim without my final papers.

My being in N.S.W. is going to make it difficult for me to prove I am the rightfull owner as I cannot claim them in person.

I also wish to know if my discharge papers are signed as ▓ my valuables are under the name of ▓ at the Public Curator's and I don't know how to explain the change of name. I don't know if you remember me or not but if you do you may be pleased to hear I am working on a sheep station 34,000 acres as housemaid I don't drink, I sleep well, and I am very happy in my job. I am writing to you personally as I know you understand my case. Hoping to hear from you soon.

Yours Truly Audrey
M. M. ▓

Letter of Congratulation
to Audrey

**Minister for Aboriginal and Torres Strait Islander Policy
and Minister for Women's Policy
and Minister for Fair Trading**

The Hon. Judy Spence MLA
Member for Mount Gravatt

2 5 AUG 1999

Ms Audrey Evans
ACACIA RIDGE QLD 4110

Dear Ms Evans,

I wish to take this opportunity to congratulate you on being named the Indigenous Scholar of the Year.

Like many other Queenslanders, I am inspired by your hard work and encouragement of others to undertake academic studies. To be honoured this way recognises your efforts and commitment to supporting the community.

It is always heartening to hear of such well deserved recognition.

I would like to draw your attention to the Register of Women. The register nominates women for positions on government boards. Your experience would be a valuable addition to the register and I have enclosed a Registration Form for your consideration.

Once again congratulations and all the best in your future endeavours.

Yours sincerely,

Judy Spence MLA
Minister for Women's Policy

Postal
PO Box 106
Albert Street
Brisbane 4002

Office
Level 18
Mineral House
41 George Street
Brisbane 4000

Telephone
(07) 3227 8819

Facsimile
(07) 3221 9964

Electorate office
20 Creek Road
Mount Gravatt 4122

Telephone
(07) 3349 9159

Facsimile
(07) 3849 5316